Lipstick Philosophy

Daily Wisdom for the Modern Woman

By

Dr. Stephanie Aldrich

Disclaimer

Although the author and publisher have made every effort to ensure that the information in this e-book was correct at press time, the author and publisher do not assume and hereby disclaim any liability to any party for any loss, damage, or disruption caused by errors or omissions, whether such errors or omissions result from negligence, accident, or any other cause.

This e-book is not intended as a substitute for the financial advice of professional financial brokers, planners, and insurance agents.

This e-book is not intended as a substitute for the medical, marital, or spiritual advice of physicians, psychologists, counselors, therapists, and clergymen. The reader should regularly consult these professionals in matters relating to their physical and mental health, particularly concerning any symptoms that may require diagnosis or medical attention.

978-1-7333770-3-4

Dedication

To my mom, sister, sister-in-laws, and girlfriends.

"Happiness is the meaning and the purpose of life, the whole aim and end of human existence."
-Aristotle

Be happy and have fun every day. Call me when it's time for a GNO!

Table of Contents

Introduction

"We do not escape into philosophy, psychology, and art–we go there to restore our shattered selves into whole ones."

–Anaïs Nin, *In Favor of the Sensitive Man and Other Essays*

Philosophy is a set of beliefs that can help us live our lives in a certain way. The Ancient Greeks and Romans used philosophy as a way to question the rules and certainty of the day. Socrates was very inquisitive and questioned everything people said and did. He challenged the logic of his day.

In modern times, we tend to spend our days being busy. We do countless chores and tasks that never move the needle. We waste our time and our energy doing things for other people. Sometimes we do these things to gain acceptance. Sometimes we do these things because they become our habitual routines. We need to wake up and challenge ourselves to question our motives. Why are we doing these things? Why are we blindly wasting our precious resources on mundane tasks that never help us lead a meaningful and fulfilled life?

This is where philosophy can help. Philosophy extends into every part of our daily lives. It questions us. It can make us think. It can open our minds to new ideas. It can challenge us. It can make us more aware. It can help us realize what's truly important to us. And doesn't that sound wonderful? Who wouldn't want a great teacher or leader to remind you of something every day? Who wouldn't want to learn and be comforted and be reassured that what they're doing matters?

Philosophy is that great teacher. Words of wisdom from people that have lived before us. The human condition hasn't changed since the beginning of time. Yes, we've advanced through technology and industry, but life's moments haven't really changed. We all fall in love. We all fall out of love. We all are betrayed. We all feel sad. We all are victorious. We all make mistakes. We all accomplish a goal. We all fail and quit. We all make a home. We all feel alone. We all exercise. We all curl up on the couch and veg out. We all have a family we love. We all forget to reach out. We all have wants and needs. We all fail to get them.

We all go through the same issues in life. Some of us accomplish more than others. Some of us have more adventures than others. Some of us love deeper and more often than others. Some of us are lucky and have things work out for us more than others. Some of us make excuses and live in our comfort zones more than others. Some of us have outer beauty where others have inner beauty. Some of us are happy at home with our kids and some of us are happy at the office slaying deals.

Our differences don't separate us. Our differences unite us. There's always another side to the coin. Some of us live on one side of the coin whereas some of us live on the other side. This doesn't mean you can't experience both sides. But you must open your mind to the other side. It will be different and it will involve making different choices and taking different actions. But that's what is exciting about life, isn't it? It's the freedom to choose something completely new and different that makes life full of adventure. But it will only be different and full of adventure if you take advantage of it. The sky truly is the limit and philosophy can help.

Philosophy is the great accumulation of wisdom. Philosophy is the written example of what everyone can feel and think. Most people never take advantage of learning history. History can show us the cause and effect of an idea or an emotion. Philosophy captures the idea and emotion in a raw form so you can make your own conclusion from it. You can take the wisdom of philosophy and use it in your own life. It can help guide you. It can comfort you. It can question your logic and motives. It can help you work out a problem. It can show you the other side of the coin. It can wake you up to other possibilities. It can help you love deeper and unconditionally. It can encourage you. It can push you out of safety and into adventure. It can bring the best out of you. It can do all of these things if you read it, embrace it, and implement it.

Philosophy is not just a bunch of words on a page. Philosophy is a way of life. Philosophy is the path that all of us can take to explore our life's purpose and give it meaning. Philosophy is a hidden truth that if implemented, can completely change your life. It can correct the smallest of behaviors. It can tackle the biggest of problems. There's no realm of life that it doesn't touch or influence.

If we take the time to read it and then apply it to our daily lives, we will find that our lives can completely change. This book is an accumulation of ancient and modern philosophical ideas that cover every area of life. From love to careers. From health to social issues. From making a difference to thinking out of the box. There's no area this book doesn't cover.

But I know you're busy. I know you have a million things on your plate today. I get it. I wear a lot of hats too. No one is busier than I am. I own my own dental practice. I am married. I have a son. I exercise. I read. I write. I have friends. I clean my own house. I cook. But in the morning, I carve out some time every day to read some philosophy. This book was inspired by *The Daily Stoic* written by Ryan Holiday. In it, he has a daily meditation from ancient philosophy. But it's written from a man's point of view. A lot of the wisdom shared in that book is meant for a man's life and not necessarily for a woman.

This is where *Lipstick Philosophy* enters the stage. Even though a lot of philosophy comes from a man's point of view, that doesn't mean we can't use it in our own way. *Lipstick Philosophy* accomplishes this task. This is an accumulation of my favorite quotes from people that I admire or have read. It encompasses different things that I have gone through or continue to go through in my own life. Because I wear many hats, I have experienced many things. I have problems and challenges ranging in different areas. I'm sure you can all relate to this. This book was written for me first, as a reminder of all the things I've experienced and finding a different way to look at those things in order to feel better about them.

Every day there's a message about something we've all experienced. *Lipstick Philosophy* will make you think. *Lipstick Philosophy* will make you cry. But in the end, *Lipstick Philosophy* will make you a better woman!

Take a few minutes every day to read the passage and write down your thoughts and feelings. Do it in the morning when your house is quiet and your mind is fresh. Then try your best to implement the thoughts and feelings that it has conjured up during your day. You'll notice by the end of the year you're a different person. Then purchase another copy for next year and start the process all over again. Through your journaling, you'll learn how you've changed your life and defeated your struggles. Through your implementation of *Lipstick*

Philosophy, you'll see clarity where you may not have seen it before. Reading, writing, and implementing it will help you create the life you've always wanted and will make you the best version you can be!

Don't take this lightly! We've only got one shot in this life as far as we know. Learn from history and build upon it. Take advantage of all that is at your fingertips. You are truly blessed to have the freedom and choices that you have in the modern world. Don't waste it! Use *Lipstick Philosophy* to spark your inner Goddess and give this gift to the rest of the world! Find your purpose and happiness and spread it to everyone you meet!

January

Hey Lady,

Today is the start of a new year. Happy New Year! Many women take this time to make a change. To improve something about their life. To create a meaningful year that they will never forget. Hopefully you already did this before the New Year, but if you didn't, today can be a start of all of those things if you take some time and dig deep. What do you want to change? What do you want to improve? We all have things that we'd love to change or improve. Today is as good of a time as any to start. For many of us, Winter is upon us and we're stuck inside, keeping warm. Why not carve out some time today to think about the things you're fed up with and want to change.? It doesn't have to be a personal manifesto, just a few things that you know you want to tackle this year. They could be big or small, it doesn't matter. The only thing that matters is that you start. Progress can only come to those that start and keep going. Take the time today and look deep inside and figure out how you want to live.

Can you do that?

Stay warm!

Stephanie

January 1st

"It's possible to start living again! See things anew as you did once, that is how to restart life!"
–Marcus Aurelius, *Meditations 7.2.*

We all get into our habitual routines. Saturdays, we clean, do laundry, and go to sporting events with our kids. We work, we cook, and we help our kids with schoolwork. Day in and day out, the same things over and over again. Remember when you were a kid? You couldn't wait to get up and start playing. Start imagining. Start pretending. What happened to that child inside of us? Even though we're adult women, we don't have to lose our curiosity. Our childlike creativity. Our playfulness. How's your marriage? Do you remember the fun you used to have with your spouse when you were first dating? The fun places you would go, and the crazy sex you'd have? When's the last time you had fun and crazy sex with your spouse? If you can't remember, then it's time to revive your inner child and renew your sense of playfulness, exploration, and fun. Everyone deserves to have fun, especially women! We do so much for other people, it's time that we start doing things for ourselves. This can include getting a massage or a pedi. Buying some lingerie and taking our spouses on a long weekend away without the kids for some hot sex and great food. What about a nice hot bubble bath listening to your favorite music uninterrupted. Whatever that is for you, make it happen this year!

How are you going to restart life and renew your spirit in the new year?

January 2nd

"You cannot escape from a prison if you don't know you're in one."
-Vernon Howard

Are you in a mental prison? Do you know you can be, have, or do anything you want? You need courage, a vision, and someone to show you the way. That's it. Too many women play the victim to society because something or someone has done them harm. Snap out of it! You are a divine spirit living in a physical body. You can do anything you want in life. Ask and ye shall receive.

Is there something you want to do or have but think you can't? Pursue it now. Don't wait. Go get it!

January 3rd

"Desiring to do something is of course a reason for doing it."

–Bernard Williams, *Ethics and the Limits of Philosophy*

If you want to make a change, you must have a strong inner desire to take the actions necessary to get the result you want. If you really want that new pair of boots, can you practice delayed gratification and save the money for it so you won't put it on a credit card? If you really want to lose weight, will you skip meeting your friends for dinner and drinks tonight so you can concentrate on your workout and diet? If you truly desire something, you can certainly have it, but there's always consequences for our desires and you must be willing to handle them when they arise.

What do you desire this year? This week? Today?

January 4th

"How much longer are you going to waste to demand the best for yourself?"
- Epictetus, *Enchiridion Manual 51*

We all procrastinate. Being a woman, we tend to do things for other people first. We help our kids with their school science project. We sewed a button on our husband's coat. We stay late to finish our group's projects. The question is, "Are you doing your best?" Sometimes we can get overwhelmed multitasking our days away. Are we busy or are we productive? Are we giving ourselves the attention we need instead of giving our attention to others? Are we growing and taking care of ourselves? Are we enjoying time every day doing something for ourselves? In order to be the best woman we can be, we must first define what that is and give ourselves the grace, time, and effort in order to become the woman we know we can become. To be the best, we must develop into her.

What are you doing today that can help you act your best?

January 5th

"Individual and social identities are created, transmitted, revised, and undermined through narratives and practices."
-Kwame Anthony Appiah, *The Politics and Ethics of Identity*

Narratives tell people who they are, how to act, and what to aspire to. This completely limits your being and puts it into a convenient, simplistic shell. But as women, we don't do things conveniently and we are far from simplistic. How you identify is how you live your life. Are you a mother? A daughter? A wife? A doctor? A teacher? An overeater? A golfer? You don't have to put yourself into any camp. I AM is one of the most powerful statements and shouldn't be taken lightly. Be very careful with what narratives you identify with. Don't ever sell yourself short. You are extraordinary! Why? Because you're a woman!

What narratives define you? Are they good and uplifting or are they bad and degrading? What bad identities can you get rid of today?

January 6th

"Discipline is giving yourself a command and following it up with action"
- Bob Proctor

How many times have you said you were going to do something, and you didn't? Most of us have experienced that. We make our New Year's resolution about losing weight, about being on time, or about getting organized. Then by February, we're right back to our old, dysfunctional habits. Discipline goes hand in hand with a clear intention. When you know why you're doing something, your intention creates the urgency to move forward and take the action necessary to get the results you're looking for. Women tend to talk about things and reiterate them over and over again without solving the problem. Without taking action. Without getting the results we're looking for. Empty talk equals empty results. You can have anything you want if you align your thoughts, feelings, and actions towards getting it. Perseverance and discipline go hand in hand. Rome wasn't built in a day. It took years and years for the reality to manifest.

What are you striving for? Better health? A better job? A loving relationship? What do you need to do to make it happen?

January 7th

"Silence isn't golden and it surely doesn't mean consent, so start practicing the art of communication."
–T.D. Jakes, *Let it Go: Forgive So You Can Be Forgiven*

Not communicating with someone can lead to negative outcomes. Whether it's your spouse, your child, your friend, or your co-worker. You will never agree with everything that people say. That's okay. But in order to move forward in your relationships, you must be able to openly communicate with other people and express your thoughts, feelings, and ideas to the world. That's what makes America a great nation built on individual's rights of freedom. To be able to communicate your feelings and thoughts openly as long as they don't harm someone else. That's the tricky part of the equation. How can we communicate our true selves with others without harming them in the process? Being honest and vulnerable is the first place to start. Listening to what the other person is saying is another. If you don't speak your mind, who will? That doesn't mean you must live in constant struggle or conflict. What it means is you take a stance when you need to. When you feel conviction. When it's necessary. And you will instinctively know when that moment is.

What can you do today to communicate your needs with someone close to you in your life?

January 8th

"A healthy man wants a thousand things, a sick man wants one."
-Confucius

Our health is the most important thing we can focus on in the new year. It should be a priority but most women let themselves go after they have kids. They get into the routines of taking care of everyone else but themselves and their health and vitality suffer from it. Change your attitude! In order to be the best mom, the best partner, the best lover, or the best employee, you must have the energy to tackle all the obstacles you will face on a daily basis. 30 minutes three times a week can help to build muscle and stamina. Intermittent fasting can help regulate metabolism and insulin levels. Eating lower carb meals and cutting your wine habit can significantly decrease your weight, allow you to sleep better, and increase your tolerance for life issues.

What can you do today to improve your health?

January 9th

"He who is not content with what he has, would not be content with what he would like to have."
-Socrates

The hedonic treadmill is the phenomenon that people return to their basic level of happiness. We want that new car. But a few months after the new car smell goes away, it's dirty, the kids have messed up the back seat, and we don't care. The thrill is gone. It's just another car to us. It's the same thing with any material thing. Once we get it, after some time, we don't even remember we have it and the excitement and anticipation slowly dissolves. Women tend to never be satisfied. That's a prison unto itself. If we're never satisfied, how can we be happy? If we're always longing for things that others have, how can we be grateful for the gift of life that we've been given? Unfortunately we can't. If we're grateful and happy with our lives the way they are, we will be grateful and happy no matter what happens and that allows us to have a fulfilled life. "Achievement without fulfillment is the ultimate failure." Tony Robbins.

What are you grateful for today?

January 10th

"So live your life wisely, not foolishly."
-The Holy Bible, Ephesians 5:15

Are you out of shape? Are you single and lonely? Do you hate your job? Are you in debt? If so, why suffer? God didn't put you on this Earth to suffer. There's thousands of years of wisdom to draw on. Whether it's The Bible, The Torah, or The Quran, someone has written about an experience they had for others to learn from. You can learn anything you want from the information on social media. YouTube alone can teach you how to get in shape, attract a loving partner, build skills to find a new job, and to live a life of financial freedom. The information and experience is out there, you must have the thirst to drink from the well.

What things must you change in your life? Where can you learn these things?

January 11th

"A writer always writes."
- Don Roff

Your identity defines your life. What you say you "are" is how you live your life. If you are a writer, you write. You write every day. You do big projects. You do small projects. If you are fat, then you're fat. You eat bad. You don't exercise. You don't care about your health. The problem with the 12 steps in Alcoholics Anonymous is that they reward themselves then they reach a certain number of days sober. If they identify as a recovering alcoholic, they will always be recovering. If they declare that they are not a drinker, then that's not something that they want to do anymore. They're not drinkers. They don't smoke. They don't eat bad food. It's their new identity. They act accordingly and get the results they're after.

What identity do you declare to the world? "I am" are the most powerful words on Earth.

January 12th

"They blossomed, they did not talk about blossoming."
-Dejan Stojanovic, *The Sun Watches the Sun*

Talking and doing are two different things.You can talk until you're blue in the face, but that doesn't change the fact that you didn't take any actions to change the situation. Fear can hold us back from moving out of our comfort zone into an unknown area. Women love certainty and consistency. We want to feel safe. We want to feel secure. But how do we change the bad things in our life if we never brave the new frontier? We need to stop talking and debating about how we're going to change our lives and start taking actions that will result in changes. Action is the only thing that will give results.

What changes do you want to make? What actions do you need to take in order to make those changes?

January 13th

"Comedy = tragedy + time."
- Carol Burnett

We all go through bad times. But as time passes, the things we thought were so awful tend to lessen. They may not sting as much. They may not make us cry as much. In some ways, they may even make us laugh. We may wonder how we got ourselves in and out of those situations in the first place. Over time, we've learned from those situations. We've gotten stronger and wiser. We've made different choices. We've done things differently. This is called experience, ladies. It comes from messing up. It comes from doing things incorrectly. It comes from failing. If we were all perfect, we'd never learn anything new. Why would we?

What hard time can we look back on and laugh?

January 14th

"When someone shows you their true colors, believe them."
-Dolly Parton

People don't change. They may put up a fake face in the beginning of a relationship. But their true personalities and values tend to come out over time. Trust their actions, not their words. Actions always speak louder. Don't tell your kids to eat better. Show them by eating well yourself and making them healthy food. If someone doesn't treat you well, change the relationship. They may apologize, but if they mess up again, trust that their actions are a reflection of their true identities and if that doesn't match your identity, walk away. Trust, but verify through action. Only through action will a true soul be revealed.

Who in your life has shown their true colors to you? Good and bad?

January 15th

"Taking care of you, doesn't mean to award yourself with a new pair of shoes or spending beyond measure on a trip to Tahiti. It actually means to take care of your financial future."
— Kim Kiyosaki, *Rich Woman: A Book on Investing for Women, Take Charge Of Your Money, Take Charge Of Your Life*

78% of Americans live paycheck to paycheck. They spend every cent that they make. They buy stuff they don't need and wonder why they never have any money. They don't budget. They think that's a waste of time and it restricts them. Yet, by the end of the month, they wonder where all their money goes because it's not assigned a role. If you want to have a secure future, and most women want security, you must start working on your finances. This means saving and investing. This means watching your spending. This means living your best life, but living it within your paycheck limits. Everyone deserves to be happy, but if your money isn't working for you, then it's making other people happy!

Write down your monthly budget:

January 16th

"One of the greatest tragedies in life is to lose your own sense of self and accept the version of you that is expected by everyone else."
-K.L. Toth

Expectations can be difficult. We often can live our lives by what we think other people think about us. What we don't understand is that people see you through your actions. If you really want to be a certain kind of person, you must act in that certain way. Then people's perception of you will align with how you see yourself. If you're living for someone else, you will never truly enjoy our life. You will never live the life you're meant to live. Create your own expectations and don't be concerned if mommy and daddy don't approve. Or if your best friend doesn't like it. So what? They're not living your life, you are. So you'd better stop living it according to them and start living it according to you.

What expectations do you have for yourself today?

January 17th

"The seed of suffering in you may be strong, but don't wait until you have no more suffering before allowing yourself to be happy."

–Thich Nhat Hanh, *The Heart of the Buddha's Teaching: Transforming Suffering into Peace, Joy, and Liberation*

There's always something. Something bad happens. Something doesn't go our way. Something doesn't work out. But that doesn't mean it should ruin our day. That doesn't mean it should ruin the progress we've made. Setbacks will always occur. Someone will always be in a bad mood. That shouldn't poison our own mood. That shouldn't interfere with our happiness. Being aware that obstacles are in front of us is called wisdom. Knowing that we'll get around them is called grace. Be happy and grateful for who you've become and what you've accomplished thus far in your life.

What makes you happy today?

January 18th

"Those who tell the stories rule society."
-Plato

Companies have their own agendas to sell you products you don't really need. They feed you a narrative that you're not good enough without their product or service. The media wants you to believe that the world is cold and unsafe. Social media wants you to blurb your unwanted opinion on every event that happens. It's all nonsense and can certainly be blocked from your consciousness. You don't have to partake in any of it. You can choose to write your own story and live by it. You can choose to be kind. You can choose to improve your environment. You can choose to educate yourself. You can choose to make a change. It's all up to us if we're going to create a fulfilling life. It's all up to us if we're going to live in a world that's wonderful. If we're listening to the negativity and brainwashing that others are filling the media streams with, then we'll never get to where we want to go. We can ignore their narratives and create our own.

What stories can you ignore today?

January 19th

"Being powerful is like being a lady. If you have to tell people you are, you aren't."
-Margaret Thatcher

We should never tell the world our business or our dreams. If we do, we can be mocked, or influenced to quit, or completely turned down a different path. The easiest way to get what we want to to live the life we desire is to do the work necessary to achieve it. We don't need anyone's permission, acceptance, or approval. If we want it, we can do it without drawing attention to ourselves. And by doing so, other people will notice. If we're only following expectations of others, how can we ever feel fulfilled? Words are worthless unless they are backed by action. Don't talk about what you're going to do or what you have already done. Be humble and show the world what you're really made from and what's deep inside you. Exude your power and your creativity with all your thoughts, words, and actions.

What actions will you take today to show others you are powerful?

January 20th

"Be strong enough to stand alone, smart enough to know when you need help, and brave enough to ask for it."
-Ziad K. Abdelnour

Everyone needs help. That's what makes the female community so strong. We talk with one another and share our wins and our losses. We confide and trust in one another. Sometimes we ask for help and sometimes we don't know we need it. We must be brave and ask others for help when we need it. That's how we grow and improve. That's how we learn what we do not know. That's how we accomplish the things that we desire. We must embrace the progress that stands in front of us and allow ourselves to be humble and ask for the things that we do not know, how to get around the obstacles that are in our way, and to meet the people that can help us during our lives. If we don't ask, we can receive. We cannot do it alone. We must help one another rise and improve our lives.

What do you need help with today?

January 21st

"At the end of the day, we can endure much more than we think we can."
-Frida Kahlo

Persistence is the name of the game for success. Fear may overwhelm us. Doubt and anxiety may try to keep us safe. We must face our fears, doubts, and anxiety and keep moving forward. We must keep trying to make our world a better place. We must use our money, our time, and our energy in improving not only our own lives, but the lives of other people. That's how strong bonds are made. That's how weak communities are improved. That's how powerful nations are built. You and I can weather any storm that comes our way. Why? Because we're strong women that want to make a difference and don't want to give up.

What problems are you trying to solve?

January 22nd

"The difference between successful people and others is how long they spend time feeling sorry for themselves."
-Barbara Corcoran

We all have bad days. We all go through rejection, failure, and defeat. But one day doesn't define us. One defeat doesn't make us a failure in life. One rejection doesn't mean we're not worthy of being loved and having a wonderful relationship. We must get up, dust ourselves off, and try again. Take a chance. Take a risk. The opposite of playing a victim. The opposite of feeling sorry for ourselves. The opposite of suffering. We must decide to take responsibility for all that happens in our lives. It's our decisions and choices that mold our outcomes. It's also our decisions and choices that keep us from moving forward. Don't allow anyone or anything to keep you from living your best life.

When have you felt sorry for yourself?

January 23rd

"Patience is bitter, but its fruit is sweet."
-Aristotle

How many times have we lost our temper? How many times have we worked and worked and worked just to get it done? How many times did we work hard to go on vacation, plan a million activities on vacation, and was even more exhausted and drained when you came back? Unfortunately, this happens continuously. We need to learn to take a break. We need to learn to enjoy the ride. We need to stop, look around, and think about something we're grateful for. We need to learn to quiet our mind, breath, and be patient. Our goal will be met. The things on our 'To Do' list will get crossed off, and we'll finally get to the end of whatever we're working on. Be patient. Enjoy the moment. Relish in the fact that you're alive and that you're in control of what's going on. Answer the questions that need to be answered and do the things that need to be done. Not in haste for the outcome, but for the purpose of knowing that you are talented enough to know the answers and to be able to get them done. Slow it down and smell the roses.

How can you show more patience today?

January 24th

"The more your money works for you, the less you have to work for money."
-Idowu Koyenikan, *Wealth for All: Living a Life of Success at the Edge of Your Ability*

76% of Americans live paycheck to paycheck. That means they are working very hard for their money. The other 24% do things the lazy way, they save enough money so they can invest it into assets that generate cash flow or appreciation. Which camp would you rather subscribe to? If you want your money working for you, you must live your life with discipline and delayed gratification. It doesn't matter if there's a sale, you're saving to invest. It doesn't matter if your friends are going out, you're saving to invest. It doesn't matter that your car is getting older, you're saving to invest. It doesn't matter that you have three roommates, you're saving money to invest. The attitude of someone that's laser-focused on the results they want are completely different from someone that's going through life with no plan. Who do you want to be?

How are you saving money today?

January 25th

"Two good talkers are not worth one good listener."
-Chinese Proverb

It's not easy to listen. It's not easy to stop and think about what someone is really saying to you. It's not easy to not give your opinion on something that you totally disagree with. But sometimes that's what's needed in the situation. Sometimes another person needs to be heard and not lectured. Sometimes it's important to stop wasting your time and energy on things that don't matter, including conversations about subjects that you don't care about. Being a good listener can make you more money if you listen to what your customer tells you and you can solve their problem with your product or service. Being a good listener can make you a better lover when you notice what your partner likes and doesn't like. Being a good listener can make you healthier when you listen to what your body is telling you about what you're eating and how you're moving. Listen to your instincts and intuitions about your life and act on them. Listen to what people are telling you and you can help them in more ways than you think.

Who can you listen to today?

January 26th

"Poor is the man whose pleasures depend on the permission of another."
–Madonna, *Justify My Love*

We tend to think that we'll be happy when that thing is over. Sometimes we'll be happy when this or that happens. Many times we think that we'll be happy when our partner does this. It's a hope and a wish when we think that the words or actions of another person can make us happy. We must feel the happiness from within ourselves. We must be satisfied with our own identity. We must be happy with our own lives. We must feel content in whatever situation we find ourselves in. We can't depend on someone else to act a certain way. We can't rely on someone else to save the day. If we lower our expectations, we can finally take a breath and feel relief. If we let things be the way they are and not have the need to form an opinion about it, we can finally relax and feel the release of our stress. Isn't that what we all want? To feel happiness on *our* terms and not someone else's? To feel satisfied that the effort we gave was good enough. To feel pride that we did things our way. To have enough in our lives. Then and only then can we find happiness without depending on the permission of someone else.

Do you need someone else's permission to be happy?

January 27th

"There's no way to be a perfect mother and a million ways to be a good one."
-Jill Churchill

The best news of all of this is that you're not expected to be a perfect mother! Phew! That's such a relief. We all want to give our children more things than what we had growing up. But the funny thing is, the only thing our children want from us is our love and attention. That's it! They want to snuggle with us. They want to play with us. They want to learn from us. They just want to be around us. That makes it so easy for us to give them what they truly want and need. Just time and attention. But even though that's simple, it's not always easy. Sometimes we have projects from work that we must finish when we get home. Sometimes we need to focus on ourselves and workout or find time to meditate. Sometimes we need to do the grocery shopping, fix dinner, and clean the house. Sometimes we have activities to attend and homework to finish. And these are legitimate things to do. But we can incorporate our children in all of these things and simultaneously accomplish our tasks and give our children what they want. It's not easy, but it's a simple solution. Involve them in your life in every way you can and you'll succeed in being a great mother.

What will you do to be a great mother today?

January 28th

"When you make a choice, you change the future."
-Deepak Chopra

Every day we make hundreds of decisions. Most of them aren't significant to the course of our lives. But once in a while we make one that completely changes the path that we're heading down. These are the exciting decisions. These are the scary decisions. These are the decisions that make you grow into the person you've always wanted to become. These decisions come with two choices. We either choose to go in a new and different direction, or we decide to stay the same. If we decide to stay the same, we'll continue getting the same average, mediocre results we've always had. But if we decide to choose something new and different, we can completely change the results we've been getting. We can choose to get into shape and eat healthy. We can choose to work smarter, not harder. We can choose to get out of debt and build wealth. We can choose to follow our dreams or we can choose to stay safe. Our choices in the present can build or hinder our futures. It's up to us to make the correct choices along the way.

What important decision can you make today?

January 29th

"Life isn't about finding yourself. Life is about creating yourself."
–George Bernard Shaw

Yesterday we made an important decision. It was our choice to make that decision. We didn't *have* to do it, but we wanted different results, so we decided to start acting differently so we could get the results we really want. Today we can take that concept a step further and realize that we can create any result we want in any area of our life. We can build the perfect life! But in order to do this, we need to take a step back and think about what we want and what we don't want. Then we must first get rid of the unwanted people, activities, and physical possessions that are keeping us from where we want to be. Then we'll have room for the things that we really want. We'll have the time we need to learn new things. We'll have the money we need to build wealth. We'll have the energy we need to implement these changes. We get rid of the old to make room for the new.

What/who do you need to get rid of ?

Where do you want to go?

What do you need to learn?

January 30th

"You can't live your life for other people. You've got to do what's right for you, even if it hurts some people you love."
-Nicholas Sparks, *The Notebook*

Making a choice to improve your life sometimes comes with consequences. Sometimes the people around you will fight with you. It's not that they want to fight with you, they are concerned and don't want to see you hurt. They don't want you to fail or even worse, to succeed and leave them behind. But in reality, you will leave them behind but that doesn't mean that you won't continue to love them. But you'll love them from a distance, and not allow them to influence you or your decisions in the future. It's important to be our own women. It's important to make educated decisions. It's important to be different. It's important to grow and improve your life. If this means that you need to go it alone, then do it. You'll find new people that are living at the same level as you want to live. You'll find new people that will support you and encourage you to continue with your growth. It's scary, but necessary to live your own life and not the life that someone expects you to live.

What kind of people do you need in your life today?

January 31st

"Well-behaved women seldom make history."
-Laurel Thatcher Ulrich, *Well-Behaved Women Seldom Make History*

Is it exciting when we play it safe? Nope, not even close. Do we grow and improve when we think the same thoughts, believe the same beliefs, and take the same actions? Nope, sounds boring! Do most of us spend our time doing the things that are expected of us? Yep, that about sums it up. We don't have to burn our bras to make history. We could pay off our debts and build wealth. That certainly could change the history of our family moving forward. We could take a chance and develop new skills and take that new job in a different city. That would certainly change the trajectory of your life. We could take a chance on a new love interest we recently found. That could certainly change the path our life takes. It's the little chances, the little risks, the little ways that we seek adventure and variety that can change our lives over the long haul. We don't have to invent some Earth-shattering product or service in order to make history. We can do small things for our families and communities that can alter their well-being. Small things can add up in big ways.

How will you make history today?

February

Hey Lady,

Think of this month as the 'Love month!" Why not focus on your heart and your body this month. Grab some of your favorite chocolate, some champagne, draw a bubble bath, and spend the night with your lover enjoying each other's bodies and souls. You don't have to go away to take a vacation. Explore your relationship this month and spend some time being grateful for the love you share with your spouse or special someone. You've a very lucky woman to have found someone to share your life with. There are many women in the world who are alone and have to navigate their lives by themselves. So be grateful! Be grateful that you're open to love and being vulnerable to someone else. Relish the fact that someone decided to live their life with you, through the good times and the bad times. Love truly is a wonderful thing!

If you don't have anyone special in your life, now is a great time to put yourself out there! Don't be afraid! That special someone could be closer than you think! Your heart and your body craves attention. Put yourself out there and see what happens! You won't regret it!

Enjoy the sensuality of Love this month!

February 1st

"Gender is by no means tied to material bodily facts but is solely and completely a social construction, a fiction, one that, therefore, is open to change and contestation: Because there is neither an 'essence' that gender expresses or externalizes nor an objective ideal to which gender aspires."

–Judith Butler, *Performative Acts and Gender Constitution: An Essay in Phenomenology and Feminist Theory*

Women face the same struggles as men. We may internalize them more. We may worry about them more. We may play victim to them. But we have just as much power as a man to solve them. To persevere. To succeed. To live the life we deserve.

How are you playing the female gender card in your life? Is it serving you or is it holding you back?

February 2nd

"When you begin to realize that your past does not necessarily dictate the outcome of your future, then you can release the hurt. It is impossible to inhale new air until you exhale the old."

–T.D. Jakes, *Healing the Wounds of the Past*

Are you holding onto sorrow from the past? We all experience hurt, pain, rejection, and physical scars. But do we have to hold onto them forever? Scars heal. Time heals the pain. Happiness replaces sorrow. Acceptance restores rejection. If you're feeling something bad, you can reach out to feel something good. The past is the past, and there's nothing you can change about it. Live today as the present because it's a gift from The Universe giving us another chance to live a fulfilled life. Today is another chance to give more to others. Today is a chance to persevere, to give our all, and to connect with as many people as we can. Anyone can improve anything they want at any time, no matter what they've failed at in their past. Why is this any different from you? Your past is not your present and it's certainly not your future. If you don't like something, change it. It won't be easy, and it won't be fun. But if you want to stop living the painful feelings of your past, you certainly can do that with a little energy and focus. Stop moving backwards and start focusing on moving forwards.

What is one thing in the past you can move on from? What steps do you need to take to bury it and create the life you want?

February 3rd

"You are not your body and hairstyle, but your capacity for choosing well. If your choices are beautiful, so too will you be."
-Epictetus

Women are characterized by our beauty. If you're beautiful on the outside, it seems the world caters to your very needs. Men and women flock to you and want to give you what you want. Society treats you differently. The downfall of outside beauty is that it fades over time. Our youthful, smooth skin slowly becomes taunt and wrinkled. Our energy dwindles. Our worth in society fades because our outside beauty fades. But as Epictetus, a former slave and philosopher said, we're not our body or our hairstyle. We are a spiritual being living in a human experience. Our spirit has no boundaries. Beauty must lie within if we are to be fulfilled in life. Our connections. Our attitude. Our actions all play a role in our beauty. If we're gracious, and loving, and giving to others, we will radiate the beauty of life and the blessings that God and The Universe have given us. If we care for others and prioritize leaving people better after we connect with them, that's beauty from within. When we make good choices, we live a good life. And that's a beautiful thing. Don't allow anyone to limit your beauty from your body. Exude your beauty through your character and your talents.

How will you show the world your inner beauty today?

February 4th

"Learn to value yourself, which means: fight for your happiness."
-Ayn Rand

Many women don't feel worthy. They're not pretty enough. They're not smart enough. They're not strong enough. Whatever inner dialogue you're telling yourself is false. You are worthy. In fact, you're more worthy of love, of success, of happiness than most people you know. You're a beautiful woman inside and out because you give so much of your time and energy to those that you love. They love you because you're so giving. Others want to spend time with you because of your talents and attitude you share with the world and they want to be a part of it. Don't allow anyone to tell you you're worth less than you know you're worth. Dig deep and fight for what you want and what you believe in. No one is more important than you. Share your thoughts and beliefs with the world and be open to learning and improving them. You can do, be, and have anything you want in this life. But it won't be easy and you will need the help of others to accomplish it. And that's okay. Ask for help and go for it. You're valuable and worthy and deserve all the happiness in the world.

What do you think about yourself? Good and bad. What can you start to improve today?

February 5th

"I'm selfish, impatient, and a little insecure. I make mistakes, I am out of control, and at times hard to handle. But if you can't handle me at my worst, then you sure as hell don't deserve me at my best."
-Marilyn Monroe

That's what a true relationship is. It's going through the good times and the bad times together. We have decided to spend our lives with each other and face whatever obstacles that come our way together. We work as a team. We're on each other's side. We help each other. We love each other. We support each other no matter what. We must give our partner's grace when they need it. Not every day will be the best, but we must love our spouse or partner no matter what. That's how relationships endure. That's how we know that we truly love someone when they show us their human side and we still love them anyway.

How can you give your spouse or partner grace today?

February 6th

"To perceive is to suffer."
-Aristotle

Our perceptions in life drive our actions and in the end, our realities. Do you easily cast opinions or judgements on something without getting all the facts? Do you side with someone without hearing the other side of the argument?When we live our lives based on opinions and hearsay, we close off the possibility of learning something new. Of reaching a new height. Of changing our mind. Of improving. Our opinions and beliefs may not be factual. We may think that we can't lose weight because we're "big boned." Or that we can't become wealthy because no one else in our neighborhood did. We may blame our circumstances on others. When we do this, we suffer. We don't live up to our potential. We don't live the life we desire and deserve. Gaining knowledge and facts over opinions can help to decrease our suffering and allow us to grow and get better.

What false perceptions do you have about your life?

February 7th

"Whining is not only graceless, but can be dangerous. It can alert a brute that a victim is in the neighborhood."
-Maya Angelou, *Wouldn't Take Nothing for My Journey Now*

Whining. Bitching. Complaining. Do you know someone that does that? Is it you? Moaning and complaining about something only insinuates that you're playing the victim role. There's only so much we can control. Why not focus on ourselves and what's in our power? Using our energy to complain about something that's not in our control is a means to disaster. Nothing will come of it. It won't make you or anyone else feel better about the situation. Instead of complaining and letting everyone around you know that you feel helpless, why don't you take a step back and figure out if there's a way for you to change the situation. If you can, stop complaining and start acting. If you can't, stop complaining and accept the situation as it is. Either way, you are free from the feeling of victimhood.

Can you stop complaining and whining today?

February 8th

"The Universe is not punishing you or blessing you. The Universe is simply responding to the vibrational attitude that you are emitting."
-Abraham Hicks

We are a magnet for our thoughts. If we're thinking positive thoughts, positive opportunities will surround us. If we're thinking and feeling negative thoughts and emotions, those are the opportunities that we'll see. It's all about our attitudes and our perceptions of our environment. If we think that nothing ever good happens to us, we'll never see the good things that are right in front of us, let alone, explore them. If we're constantly moaning and bitching about our situation, we'll never take the action necessary to change it for the better. It all starts and ends with us. We need to stop playing the victim of our circumstances and start taking responsibility for it.

How can we put out good vibes today?

February 9th

"Some women choose to follow men, and some women choose to follow their dreams. If you're wondering which way to go, remember that your career will never wake up and tell you that it doesn't love you anymore."
-Lady Gaga

How many celebrities or close friends do you know are successful but yet, their spouses or lovers cheat on them or leave them? It's very important to have our own careers and activities that fulfill us. We should never depend on someone else to make us happy or to support us financially. If we do, we give all of our power to them to do with what they want. This leaves us dependable on them and vulnerable. No woman should be dependable or vulnerable to anyone! If someone truly loves you, they will support and love you as you follow your dreams and ambitions. They will fight for you and be there for you when you've hit an obstacle. When they decide to part ways with you, if they do, you know deep down that you're strong enough and that you can take care of yourself. Never give up on your dreams or hand over your power to control your life to someone else.

How can you keep control of your life?

February 10th

"Love is like the wind, you can't see it, but you can feel it."
-Nicholas Sparks, *A Walk to Remember*

Love is an emotion that can overwhelm us. It can drive our sexual desire. It can create compassion within us. It can give us energy and focus on what we want. Love can bring out the best and worst in us. It can create happiness and sadness. It can cause anger and grief. It can make us love someone unconditionally. Love can be felt for a child, a family member, or a lover. It spans every part of our life. It weaves itself in every thought and every action. It can support us through tragedy. It can lift us to Heaven. We can see love if we look at the actions of other people. When we help each other and support each other, there is love. When you see families and communities, there is love. When you see smiling faces and laughter, there is love. Love is all around us and we should be grateful for it each and every day.

Where do you see love?

February 11th

"There are two basic motivating forces: fear and love. When we are afraid, we pull back from life. When we are in love, we open to all that life has to offer with passion, excitement, and acceptance."
-John Lennon

Women tend to be shy. We tend to sit back and stay in our comfort zones. But that's not where love lives. That's not where life can be lived. We must break out of our shells and find the drive to make our dreams come true. We must thirst for love and allow that thirst to encourage us to move on. We must open our hearts to other people. We must trust that things will work out for us. When we love ourselves, we can find love in the world. If we're always fearful and reserved, we close ourselves off from feeling and experiencing all the wonderful things and people that the world has to offer us.

Will you be fearful or full of life and love today?

February 12th

"Contentment is natural wealth, luxury is artificial poverty."

-Socrates, *Essential Thinkers*

Knowing what enough is, is the most satisfying and freeing feeling you can have in your life. When you are in your 20s, you work hard, get promoted, and climb the corporate ladder. You may find love and start a family. You start multitasking to get everything done that you think you must do each and every day until you come to a point where you're exhausted both physically, mentally, and emotionally. Burnout amongst women is a true thing and must be dealt with early before you break down. Look around now and realize that you are enough. How much money you have is enough. Your family is enough. How many pairs of shoes you have is enough. Stop running on the hamster wheel trying to accumulate more, more, and more because you've compared yourself to someone else who has more. Would you rather have less and be free from the daily grind and the upkeep to all of those possessions? Buying physical possessions only gives us a short term dopamine and serotonin rush that quickly fades away. Why not have satisfaction long term by realizing that what you have, who you're with, and who you are is enough.

Do you know what enough is in your life?

February 13th

"A good apology has three parts:

1. I am sorry.
2. It's my fault.
3. What can I do to make it right?

Most people forget the third part.
-Abdul Kalam

Admitting that we're wrong is never an easy thing to do. But everyone goes through it. We're not perfect. We're women and we're doing the best we can with what we have. Sometimes things work out, and sometimes we mess up. That's what makes life interesting. It's in the times that we mess things up that we learn our greatest lessons. That's how we grow and improve our lives. Especially when we're learning something new. Of course, we won't do it right the first time. Of course, we'll get the answers wrong. But we need to practice grace and humility and ask questions to those that are wiser to help us figure things out for ourselves. Admitting you're wrong and then doing what's necessary to make things right is the enlightenment that you need to live a life on the right path.

Is there something you need to apologize about today?

February 14th

"I can teach you a love potion made without any drugs, herbs, or special spell. If you would be loved, love."
–Seneca from *Moral Letters 9.6.*

Over half of the world are men. That means that for every woman, there's a mate in the world that's waiting for you. If you are a lesbian, then the number is smaller, but still significant. But you can't be desperate for a relationship. Others can smell the desperation on you. ½ of all marriages end in divorce. There are many factors that factor into relationships and why some work and some don't. The best advice to finding love is this: Start with yourself first. Make yourself the best possible version. Work on your career. Work on your personality. Work on your body. Work on your strength and perseverance. When you're a strong woman, others will notice and be attracted to your strength. Help others openly. When your arms are open, someone will notice and want to feel that love. Before you get love, show love. It works the same for anything. Want more money? Give more money. Want more love? Give more love to others. What you give, you will receive.

How will you show love to others today?

February 15th

"In the end, you have to choose whether or not to trust someone."
-Sophie Kinsella, *Shopaholic & Baby*

Trust is difficult for some people. When we are young, we trust that our parents will keep us safe. As we get older, we develop trust through friendships and our first lovers. But most of the time, those friendships and relationships end and can cause pain and strife in our lives. These experiences can cause baggage that we carry with us. Sometimes this baggage can interfere with us trusting other people and situations. Sometimes this baggage can make us doubt ourselves. Sometimes this baggage can make us feel unworthy of love or success. The only way to move on is to drop the excess baggage and start believing that we are enough. We are wonderful, beautiful, and worthy of being loved and of being successful. If other women can do it, why can't we? Everyone has bad experiences but we can't allow those experiences to stop us from living the life we want and deserve. This includes being loved and finding success.

How can you build trust with someone today?

February 16th

"Nobody has ever measured, not even poets, how much the heart can hold."
-Zelda Fitzgerald

It's amazing how wonderful we are. Our hearts are so large that we can fit the love we have for our friends, our families, our lovers, and other women. We have compassion. We empathize with others. We nurture the next generations with our love and kindness. We can look on the positive side and always give the benefit of the doubt. We can love unconditionally. We can hope and dream for a better tomorrow. We can voice our opinions and use our talents for the good of the community. We are wonderful women and we should remind ourselves of our power and capacity for love.

What do you love?

February 17th

"Love doesn't just sit there, like a stone, it has to be made, like bread; remade all the time, made new."
-Ursula K. Le Guin, *The Lathe of Heaven*

Sometimes our relationships become stale. We do the same things and get in a rut. There's no spark. There's no excitement like when we first met. We're bogged down with our daily routines, work, and children. We have no energy or creativity to think of fun things to do with our lovers. It's the same ol' thing, day after day until one day we wake up, look at our partner, and realize we don't love them anymore. It's not that we don't love them anymore, it's that we've neglected our relationship. We need to actively rejuvenate our love we have for them. We must be active in keeping the spark alive. We must carve out time and energy for sex, for intimacy, and for having some fun together. That's what it was like in the beginning and that's what it should be like today. Nourish your relationship and treat it like a living soul. Pay attention to it and give it what it needs to flourish and succeed.

How can you spark your relationship today?

February 18th

"Always be a first-rate version of yourself, instead of a second-rate version of someone else."
-Judy Garland

We are bombarded with advertisements and marketing messages every day telling us how desperate we are. We're desperately seeking beauty, health, wealth, and physical possessions. And of course, those companies who pay the marketing agencies play on those emotional wants. But what if we knew that deep down we didn't need any of that stuff? What if we knew deep down that we were already beautiful, healthy, and wealthy and that we didn't need to prove it to anyone else. What if we were already happy with what we've accomplished in our lives? What if we lived each and every day the way we wanted? We all have unique gifts and talents. What if we shared them with the world? What if that's all we needed to do to be successful and fulfilled? What if we strived to be the best version of ourselves each and every day? What if we paid attention to loving ourselves and loving all those around us? Don't you think that would make a difference? Don't you think that would solve a lot of problems that we see? If we concentrate on being our best self, we would have the energy to help others be their best selves. And if everyone lived up to their potential, wouldn't this world be a better place?

How can I be my best self today?

February 19th

"I've been absolutely terrified every moment of my life, and I've never let it keep me from doing a single thing I wanted to do."
-Georgia O'Keeffe

Fear always protects us from the unknown. Fear always keeps us safe. Fear always keeps us in our comfort zone. But where's the fun in that? Where's the adventure? Where's the growth? Where's the contribution? In order to live a successful and meaningful life, we must learn what we don't know. We must meet new people. We must be open to new and different ideas. We must learn new skills and ways of thinking. We must take new and challenging actions. When we let go of our fears, we open a new world of opportunities and possibilities. When we let go of our fears, we're able to progress, find love, and find meaning in our lives. When we let go of our fears, we start having fun adventures. Doesn't that sound exhilarating? Doesn't that draw you towards something new? Doesn't that excite your curiosity? Doesn't that make you feel alive? Let go of the fear that keeps you bored and miserable and open yourself up to new and different people and things.

What adventure do you want to start today?

February 20th

"We accept the love we think we deserve."
–Stephen Chbosky, *The Perks of Being a Wallflower*

Why should love be any different than anything else? We live by our standards. We accept what we *think* we deserve. Our identities are defined by our self-worth. If we don't feel worthy of finding love, we never will find it. We can never open ourselves up to another person if we have doubts about ourselves. It takes courage to take a risk in the love department. What if we're rejected? What if we fail to meet their expectations? In love, we need to be open to whatever the wind blows in our path. Sometimes the opportunities will work out, and sometimes they won't. But that's what makes life exciting. It's the adventure and taking the risk on the unknown that's the spice of life.

Do you think you deserve love?

February 21st

"Never love anyone who treats you like you're ordinary."
-Oscar Wilde

You are wonderful! You are a very special woman! You're beautiful, loving, and full of spunk. You deserve to have a wonderful partner to share your life with. If your lover isn't treating you well, either try to fix it, or get rid of them. You deserve the best and if you're not feeling the love, go find someone that deserves you. You're extraordinary and your partner should acknowledge that fact. There's a yang for every ying. There's someone out there that's perfect for you. Don't settle for second best! Keep searching until you find your soulmate. Nothing else is worth living for.

Have you found your soulmate?

February 22nd

"They say everyone needs just three things to be truly happy in this world: someone to love, something to do, and something to hope for."
-Tom Bodett

We all want to live successful fulfilling lives. In order to do that, we must first think about ourselves. We must be selfish in the fact that we need to know what it is that makes us happy. We must concentrate on our health. We must concentrate on our career and finances. We must concentrate on our mental state and attitude. When we have all three of those things covered, then we can look towards finding love in the outside world. But if we don't handle the inside, selfish things first, then we can never find and appreciate the love that someone else can offer us. Once we find someone we can build a life together, we can create the goals we want to accomplish together, as a loving team. It's always easier to win with a team and your relationship should focus on working towards your common goals together, balancing each other's weaknesses and strengths. That brings hope, satisfaction, and fulfillment to your life when you know where you're going and you can do it with someone you love.

What things do you still have to work on?

February 23rd

"No relationship is perfect, ever. There are always some ways you have to bend, to compromise, to give something up in order to gain something greater. The love we have for each other is bigger than these small differences."

–Sarah Dessen, *This Lullaby*

Isn't it a relief that we don't have to be perfect? If you're a woman that strives to do everything and be everything to everyone, today you're off the hook. You can now breathe and focus on improving yourself and your weaknesses. You can work on your strengths and goals. If you're stronger and more open minded, you'll find your relationships will become better and stronger. When you put yourself in the other person's shoes and try to understand them instead of judging them, you'll be less irritable and less critical of the things they do or say. You'll find that they're more drawn to you if you don't nag them. They'll want to help you and support you and fix your problems if you open your arms to them and accept them for who they are. Together, you'll find the way.

What differences do you have with your partner or spouse?

February 24th

"I used to think that the worst thing in life was to end up alone. It's not. The worst thing in life is to end up with people who make you feel alone."
-Robin Williams

How many women do you know who are taking antidepressants but who are still depressed? Is it really a chemical imbalance or is it a spiritual, relationship imbalance? Most people who are depressed are depressed because they're not living the life they want to live. They aren't around people that support them or love them. They have no adventure and no ambition to set goals and strive to achieve them. This is a very sad way to live, and it's a complete waste of time. Stop wasting time and start living the life you want. It's not difficult to make a change. It's not difficult to learn something new, something exciting, something that can move the needle to better finances, health, and love. But it's very important to have people around you that can support you when you need it. Everyone needs help, whether it's advice on decision making, physically being able to fix something, or helping them learn a new skill set. But you have to leave your ego at the door and ask for help from those that know what to do. You've got to open your mind and accept the new ideas and actions that you're being taught. When you find something that excites you, you'll never feel alone or depressed again. But it takes inner strength to ask for help and push yourself beyond your comfort zone. You can do it!

Are there people in your life that can help you?

February 25th

"Love is that condition in which the happiness of another person is essential to your own."
-Robert A. Heinlein, *Stranger in a Strange Land*

Love can be between two people romantically. Love can be someone helping and giving money or time to another person. Love can be between a mother and her child. Love can be between two girlfriends. There are so many ways we can love other people and what's so great about love is that it is unconditional and never ending. As women, we are naturally full of love and charity. We nurture. We help. We listen. We create. Love fills our cup when we help others fill their own. Our lives have meaning and purpose when we build up others instead of tearing them down. When we give our love, we get some much more in return and that's a beautiful thing!

How can you show someone love today?

February 26th

"The truth is, unless you let go, unless you forgive yourself, unless you forgive the situation, unless you realize that the situation is over, you cannot move forward."
— Steve Maraboli, *Unapologetically You: Reflections on Life and the Human Experience*

Forgiveness is never easy. If someone has wronged you, you feel hurt, ashamed, and angry. But that hurt and anger will only cause you more grief if you hold onto it and allow it to grow and strangle your purpose and meaning in life. As women, we also hold onto mistakes that we make and allow them to shadow all of the good things we do in our lives. We have to stop this behavior. We must forgive ourselves first, then forgive others and move on. We must never allow anyone or anything to hold us back from living the lives we truly want. We must be free mentally and emotionally to work on our goals and accept the people's love and support around us. We can't be cold and bitter. We must open the floodgates of love, acceptance, and appreciation. This is the only way we can move on and live a meaningful and fulfilled life.

What wrong has happened to you? Can you forgive and move on?

February 27th

"Love never dies a natural death. It dies because we don't know how to replenish its source. It dies of blindness and errors and betrayals. It dies of illness and wounds."
-Anais Nin

Love is a spiritual thing. It must constantly be nourished. It must constantly have attention and focus. If it's constantly ignored, it will go somewhere else. Like energy in our body, we feel love in our hearts. Love makes us smile. Love makes us work hard. Love makes us care for someone else above even ourselves. Love is a truly magical thing. What's great about love is we can create it anytime we want. If we meet someone we know that we want to spend more time with, we create new love and affection for that person. When our partner does something nice for us, we're reminded of the love that we felt for them in the beginning of our relationship. When our child is sick, we feel the love that we have for them and want to care for them and make them better. All of this love is inside us. We get to enjoy it and express it when we decide that the world needs us and that we're willing to share ourselves with them. We can create love anytime we want and we must make sure we're constantly resupplying that energy to our relationships so they can be nourished and continue to grow.

How can you nourish your relationships today?

February 28th

"Too often we underestimate the power of a touch, a smile, a kind word, a listening ear, an honest accomplishment, or the smallest act of caring, all of which have the potential to turn a life around."
— Leo Buscaglia

It's the small things that count. It's the small things that add up to our overall nature. It's the small things we need to focus on each day. We can't do huge monumental things every day. But we can do the small things. A hug. A compliment. A smile. A note of flirtation. Making some cookies for your kids. Giving a shoulder rub to your partner. It's those little things we can do everyday to let the people we love know that we're thinking of them and that they still matter to us. Being aware of your loved ones presence and showing them that you care can mean all the difference to them. Making a cup of coffee and talking with your spouse about their day. Sitting down at the kitchen table and helping your child with their homework. Sending a funny meme to your girlfriend that will make her laugh. Saying thank you. Giving a wink. All of these things add up to a meaningful attitude and way of life.

What small thing can you do today to show your loved ones they are loved?

February 29th

"Boredom is the biggest problem. The same position. Same day of the week. It becomes boring when you don't bring any added flowers home."
-Dr. Ruth Westheimer

We all get in routines with our partner. Some of it is good, but other times, it gets pretty boring. Why not spice things up? Watch a video together. Go to the adult store and buy a toy or some lingerie. Leave the kids with your mom and go on a weekend getaway with your lover and have only one thing in mind- sex. Did you forget that you're a sexual goddess? Did you forget that you are still attracted to your spouse? When was the last time you had an orgasm? When was the last time you did it in the laundry room or the kitchen? Raising children and having careers can wear us down. Make time for a healthy sex life. Your sex goddess will thank you.

How can you spice things up tonight?

March

Hey Lady,

Spring is right around the corner. With the change of the season can come a change in your life. Why not dust off those goals and resolutions you've put away in the drawer. Now is a great time to work on what you want out of this year. It's never too late to start! Think about it, you could be a whole different person by the end of the year if you decide to start. That's all you have to do, just start. Take the first step today in whatever you want to do.

Do you want to lose weight? Do you want to move? Do you want to look for a new job? Do you want to be debt free? Today is a great day to focus on what you really want out of life and start the journey towards accomplishing it.

You can do it! Take the first step today!

March 1st

"One of the secrets of a happy life is continuous small treats."
-Iris Murdoch

The Stoic philosophy is to live in moderation. That means to avoid extremes on both ends. Treating oneself occasionally is a must. Whether it's your favorite chocolate. Or it's your favorite pair of jammies. Or even a massage or a facial. Small occasional treats are self indulgent and can help to give you a boost of dopamine and serotonin that you need to get through your busy schedule. Nowadays women are going, going, gone. All the time, not stopping until you crash in bed. Then you get up and do it all over again the next day. It's a great thing to treat yourself to something you love. It doesn't have to be anything expensive or extravagant or time consuming. Just something that you love and that makes you feel alive and happy about that moment. Watch your favorite movie. Take a hot bubble bath with scented candles. Order your favorite takeout. Do something today that brings a smile to your face and warmth to your heart.

What can you do today to treat yourself?

March 2nd

"There is a difference between being poor and being broke. Broke is temporary. Poor is eternal."

-Robert Kiyosaki, *Rich Dad Poor Dad*

Being poor is a mindset. It's a way of thinking. Most people on welfare raise children that end up on welfare. Why? Because it's the ideas and beliefs of victimhood that are infused in their children's minds. They think that they have nothing to contribute to society, that they were born in poverty so that's their lot in life. Having no money can change easily with education, mentorship, and a positive mindset. You must work hard. You must persevere. You must step out of your comfort zone and pursue ideas and actions that you've never attempted before. That's the only way to stop the poor mentality. That's the only way to stop being broke. If you change your attitude, you'll change your life!

What can you do today to make some money?

March 3rd

"The serpent, if it wants to become the dragon, must eat itself."
-Sir Francis Bacon

We may say we want to change, but do we really want to do what's needed to make the change? Do we want to put in the blood, sweat, and tears necessary to take the next step? Do we want to spend our resources of money, time, and energy in order to take our lives to the next level? In order to do that, we must change our identity. I am husky, therefore I can't lose weight because of my identity. I come from a poor family, therefore I can't become wealthy is another identity. Whatever your identity is that you're telling yourself needs to change. It needs to die. In order for your new identity to velcro itself to your life, you need to lay to rest the old identity and all the excuses and obstacles that go along with it. Once you identify with something new, you will start acting the part. You will start exercising and eating well. You will start learning new skills that can get you a better job and increase your wealth accumulation. It's the new identity that can give you the life you want, not the old one. If the old one had that power, it would already be delivering the success you want.

What is your current identity? What is your new identity that will help you succeed?

March 4th

"I've always hated the "Who are you?" question. This is a philosophical inquiry. Answering that question is why we're on earth. You can't answer it in thirty seconds or in an elevator."
-Sandy Nathan, *Numenon*

We're women. We're complicated. We wear a lot of hats and identify with a lot of characters. How can you sum up your life's work in a word or a few sentences? You can't. And the reason you can't is because your identity can depend on the time the question was asked. Are you a mother yet? Are you a wife or partner yet? Are you middle aged yet? Are you a doctor? Are you healthy yet? Are you wealthy yet? Your main identity is built brick by brick throughout your life and at any time, those bricks may change. You may not stay a career woman forever. A teacher. A computer analyst. You may not be raising a family. Those bricks are built layer by layer as your life proceeds. Some of them will stick, while others will be replaced by bigger and better identities. One thing you can never deny, is that you're a woman and you have a place on this Earth.

What do you identify with at this point in your life?

March 5th

"I strive for perfection - I settle for satisfaction."
- Carroll Bryant

As women, we tend to wrap ourselves in the notion that we must be Superwoman. We need to be the best in the boardroom, raise perfect children, and satisfy our hot spouses when we get home. But how realistic is this? Not much. It's okay to strive for progress, but perfection is something that is never attainable. You can't be everything to everyone at the same time. Sometimes you must say no. Sometimes you won't be able to do that activity. Sometimes you will need help to complete something. It's okay. Give yourself a break and let yourself off the hook. No one expects you to be perfect. No one expects you to get everything done. The only person that's holding the cards is you. And you can play any of them that you choose.

What can you say 'no' to today?

March 6th

"Every time you spend money, you're casting a vote for the kind of world you want."
-Anna Lappe

Most women love to shop. But what we don't realize is that shopping is an important responsibility. We alone can shape the world with the items that we purchase. If we don't want sugary cereals to make our kids fat, why not stop buying them? If we want to increase our wealth, why are we spending our extra money on frivolous material goods instead of saving it and investing it? The way we spend our money matters. It shapes regulations that govern industry. It shapes what products are manufactured. What we do matters. It matters to us and it matters to our future. Don't waste it on material goods that don't improve our lives and make a change for the better. Corporations change when revenues decrease. Make your voices heard by using your wallet.

What can you do to be more intentional with your spending?

March 7th

"Wealth is an attitude. If you feel like you're so happy and so content with what you have, you are already wealthy."
– Ken Honda

If you love what you do, money will flow to you. If you help people solve their problems, money will flow to you. If you network with successful people, money will flow to you. If you seek opportunities and don't wait for them to happen to you, money will flow to you. If you take the right actions in the right way, money will flow to you. Money is energy and it goes where the energy goes. If you're creating a positive energy and are consistently helping others, you are emitting money energy and money will be attracted to you. Being wealthy and being rich are two different things. Being grateful for what you have and who you've become makes you the richest woman on Earth, no matter how much money you have. But it's always nice to have some extra money in the bank.

What can you do today to make more money?

March 8th

"Someone's sitting in the shade today because someone planted a tree a long time ago."
-Warren Buffett

We must plan for the future. The seeds you plant today can give you years of shade later in life. Save and invest money and allow compounding interest to bless your account. Spend time with your children and teach them good habits. This will help them become successful productive adults later in life. Eat healthy today and get in a good workout. If you do this consistently, you will find that you feel healthy and you look great in your skinny jeans. If you build your network of customers over time, you'll find increasing opportunities that turn into sales. Taking each day and maximizing your opportunities, increases your chances of finding wealth, success, and happiness.

What seed are you planting today that will benefit you in the future?

March 9th

"Be courteous to all, but intimate with few, and let those few be well tried before you give them your confidence."
-George Washington

Having a broad social network is important to having a successful career. But keeping your inner circle small and intimate is also very important. When your inner circle is small, your morals and values can remain your own. There's not a lot of distractions and outside influences that can derail your friendships. Trust takes time to build and not everyone you meet is trustworthy. What are their intentions? What do they want from you? Will they keep your trust or break it? Will they try to sabotage you? Will they help and support you when you need them? Very few people will be there for you when your world comes crashing down. Sometimes you will go through bad times. Your true girlfriends will be the women that stand beside you. Women who will hold your hand and cry with you. Women who will tell you the truth even though it may hurt. Women who will be honest with you. Women that love you. Those are the women that you can trust. Those are the women who are in your corner backing you up.

Who is in your inner circle?

March 10th

"Don't be intimidated by what you don't know. That can be your greatest strength and ensure that you do things differently from everyone else."
-Sara Blakely

No one needs permission to ask a question. No question is stupid. If you're afraid to ask a question, then you're not really interested in finding the answer. If you want a specific result, you'll ask others how to get there and in return, you'll find your way. We all start from ground zero. We can't hit the ball when we start playing golf or tennis. But with a coach, we can learn the fundamentals. We all start in entry-level jobs after college. But through skill building and networking, opportunities to grow in our career happen. We all start with little money, but we learn how to build our wealth by reading, listening to podcasts, and watching our investments. Never be afraid to ask questions and learn new things. That's the only way we grow and improve.

What question can I ask someone today?

March 11th

"You must not lose faith in humanity. Humanity is an ocean; if a few drops of the ocean are dirty, the ocean does not become dirty."
-Mahatma Gandhi

Times today are rough. The politicians are all corrupt. Racism floods the streets. Wars and death are in the media. Poverty and suffering are everywhere. The world looks like it's coming to an end. Or does it? Even though there's bad things and bad people in the world, not everyone or everything is bad. You're a good person. You try your best to have a good life. You give to your community and church. You're loving and care about your friends and family. You're positive and spread your attitude with everyone you meet. You are successful and won't allow anyone or anything to get in your way. You're a badass and you know it! Don't let the negativity weigh you down. There's always going to be issues in the world. Make sure the world you live in, your home, your community, your network is made of good things and good people. Goodness always prevails.

What good things are in your life?

March 12th

"Change equals self improvement. Push yourself to places you haven't been."
-Pat Summitt

Women like comfort and security. But to improve your situation, you must make a change. And to make a change requires some discomfort. You'll go through some pain. You'll go through some adversity. You'll go through some challenges. But once you go through your hardships, you'll wake up and realize you did it. You succeeded in what you were striving for. You accomplished your goal. Then all of the pain and suffering you went through along the way will fade and the feelings of victory and pride will exude from every cell of your body. You did it! You didn't give up! You found a way to get through the obstacles to the other side. The victory side. The successful side. How does it feel? Now it's time for the next challenge!

What change must you start making today?

March 13th

"If you can dance and be free and not be embarrassed, you can rule the world."
-Amy Poehler

Too many women care about what others think of them. They are forced to act a certain way and have certain things in their lives. They are expected to have certain careers and marry certain types of people. Where's the freedom in that? What makes us free is doing what we want, not caring what others think or feel about us. That doesn't mean that we can intentionally hurt other people by our actions, but if we're doing what makes us happy and fulfills our mission in life, then we shouldn't care if others have opinions about us. People will talk about us no matter what we do, so why not live our best life? Would you rather people be jealous or pitiful of you? Would you rather people be inspired or disappointed by you? The freedom sword has two edges, either way you're going to get cut. But that cut is worth it and will heal quickly if you follow your dreams and not allow others to stop you.

What makes you happy?

March 14th

"You can be gorgeous at thirty, charming at forty, and irresistible for the rest of your life."
-Coco Chanel

Being charming and gorgeous are subjective characteristics and can't be measured, but many people rely on them to help boost their self worth. What one thinks and what one does is what is most important. Those things can be measured by what kinds of results you get. It all comes down to self confidence. When you're confident, other people are drawn to you. Most women crave certainty and safety and if you exude that, they will be drawn to you. They will want to work for you because they are confident that you are confident. And in that confidence comes the safety and security they want. Why not be charming, gorgeous, and confident? Why not tell the world who you are, what you're about, and show them you're a force to deal with? By doing this, you align your thoughts, actions, and feelings with that of being successful and the Universe will line up the path for you to take. Show confidence that success will come and you will be shown opportunities that will make it happen.

How can you show self confidence today?

March 15th

"I do believe that in order to be a successful negotiator, as a diplomat, you have to be able to put yourself into the other person's shoes. Unless you can understand what is motivating them, you are never going to be able to figure out how to solve a particular problem."
-Madeleine Albright

This is called the sales process. You can make as much money as you want if you can help other people solve their problems. If you have a product or service that can help the other person, they will pay you the amount of money you're asking them to pay if the problem is big enough to solve for them. You don't have to be slimy or dishonest with the person. All you have to do is connect with them and their pain and show them a better life. If you can take away their pain, they will be your loyal customer forever. This is also called empathy. If you can understand what the other person is going through and you can put yourself in their shoes, you can easily connect with them on a higher level. In that connection you can help them get to where they want to go.

How can you empathize with someone today?

March 16th

"Nothing is impossible, the word itself is- I'm possible!"
-Audrey Hepburn

Anything is possible. There are infinite outcomes to every action. Sometimes things will work out, and sometimes they won't, but there's always the possibility of success. Hope gives us the courage and the security to feel as if things will work out. But hope is not enough to make it happen. We must put in order the events that lead to the correct conclusion. We do this by creating the desired result, and working backwards to find the right path to take. It's the action that creates the outcomes, not just the hope or dream or wish. It's the courage to take that first step and then the next afterwards that propels us forward and onto greater and greater horizons. If things weren't possible, no one would be enjoying success. Our civilization would have crumbled thousands of years ago. Scientific breakthroughs would never be discovered. It's in the possibilities that progress is made. It's in the possibilities that give us ambition that drives us to improve and grow.

What is possible for you today?

March 17th

"It is what we make out of what we have, not what we are given, that separates one person from another."
- Nelson Mandela

Not everyone grows up with wealth and money. Not everyone has good health. Not everyone is smart enough to do well in school. That doesn't mean that we can't succeed. Maybe we're good at graphic design but aren't good at English. Maybe we're good at fixing things or making music. Maybe we have our beauty or are as strong as an ox. Whatever our hidden talents are, we should embrace them and create a life showcasing them. Some people work on their weaknesses to make themselves better. Why not work on your strengths and become the best in that space? More money, fame, and fulfillment can be had from using your true talents to your potential. Focus on what you love and what you're great at and leave the rest behind. You can always hire someone to handle the things you aren't good at. Focus on what you are good at and build a life on that.

What are your hidden talents?

March 18th

"Sometimes when we are generous in small, barely detectable ways it can change someone else's life forever."
-Margaret Cho

It's the little things that matter. The compliments you give can really spark someone's belief in themselves. The talents you share with the world can help to solve today's problems. The love you show someone can help them feel warm and fuzzy inside. It's the little things done consistently that can build upon themselves and can grow into a meaningful relationship. When we give, we show others our inner strength. When we give, we help our own confidence in what we're sharing. Whether it's our time, our energy, our skills, or our money, our giving helps solidify our belief in the world's abundance. There's enough for everyone and charity helps to show it.

How can you help someone today?

March 19th

"Yesterday is history, tomorrow is a mystery, today is God's gift, that's why we call it the present."
- Joan Rivers

The only thing we can control is today. Our thoughts, our feelings, and our actions. What's our intention for today? What's our plan? Who will we see? What will we do? Are we taking any actions towards our goals? Are we working on our health? Are we working on our relationship? Are we networking with anyone new? Are we continuing to read and learn new things? Are we sticking to our budget so we can invest for our future? Today's activities can directly influence the results we get tomorrow. Don't waste your precious resources on things that don't help you live your best day. Be intentional today. Make the most of it. Create a list of activities that must get done and take some time to enjoy the people you love. There's always time for that. Work on your mission and follow the path you've created.

What are your plans today?

March 20th

"If opportunity doesn't knock, build a door."
- Milton Berle

Some women are lucky. They meet the right person. They are born beautiful. Their family is wealthy. They always seem to be in the right place at the right time. Are they really lucky, or do they put themselves in the right position to take advantage of opportunities that are presented to them? You know, you can do the same thing. If you don't feel like you're a lucky person, learn how to create your own luck. Start networking with people that have the opportunities that you're looking for. Start learning the skills that are needed to get the new job or promotion. Move to the part of the country that is looking for your talents. Invest your money so you can create financial independence. Success doesn't happen in a moment. It's intentionally created with strategic moves. You can make any move you want if you know what outcome you want to create. Make the most with what you have and keep moving towards what you want.

What opportunity can you take advantage of today?

March 21st

"It isn't events themselves that disturb people, but only their judgments about them."

-Epictetus, *Enchiridion Manual 5*

Our perceptions and opinions shape our lives. If you think about it, things aren't big nor small, tall nor short, or far or near. It is what it is. If something costs $3000, some people will think that $3000 is a lot of money but others will think it's not. Why? It's because some people would value their $3000 more than the item where others will value the item more than their money. If you get divorced, is it a curse or is it a blessing? One person may play the victim to her spouse leaving her and become desperate, needing money and support from her ex. Another woman would realize that she played a role in the marriage dissolving and would take the opportunity to work on the things that she could improve. She could get in shape, get a promotion at work, and start dating better-matched people. It's all how you look at things that influences your reactions to life issues.

Do you really need to create an opinion or judgment about this issue? What is one thing you can forgo an opinion about today?

March 22nd

"Attitude is a choice. Happiness is a choice. Optimism is a choice. Kindness is a choice. Giving is a choice. Respect is a choice. Whatever choice you make makes you. Choose wisely."

-Roy T. Bennett, *The Light in the Heart*

Every decision we make is a choice. It's either positive or negative. Every choice builds on itself and creates the path our life travels down. When we come to a decision, we must choose which course of action we're going to take. We may choose to follow the crowd and get mundane results. Or we may choose to live differently and follow the path of the successful few. The choice is always up to us but we need to realize that every choice we make can either help us live the life we desire or it will hold us back.

What path will you choose to travel down today?

March 23rd

"I'd rather regret the things that I've done than regret the things I haven't done.
-Lucille Ball

Many of us waste our days doing mundane, busy activities that don't move the needle. These activities waste our energy, our time, and often our money. Then we wonder where our resources go when we need them the most. Is this how you want to continue living your life? Spending the only life you have doing things that don't fulfill you. Things that don't make you happy. Are you living your best life? Is it full of adventure and fun? Are you surrounded by friends and loved ones? Do you have a career that fills you with purpose and drive? Are you giving back and sharing your resources with your communities? Are you traveling and seeing new parts of the world and enjoying different and exciting cultures and cuisine? If not, why? Live with no regrets and fill your days with things you love and things that challenge you to live to your potential.

Do you regret the things you haven't done? What are they?

March 24th

"The reason why we have two ears and only one mouth is so we might listen more and talk less."
- Diogenes

Many women gossip. Many women talk behind others backs. Many women lie. The world of gossip is a dangerous place to be. It can degrade beliefs and stifle positive attitudes. It can sour friendships and destroy inner circles and trust. We must rise above idle gossip and start to listen to our fellow women. Of their concerns. Of their worries. Of their obstacles. Only by listening can we band together and solve our fellow women's needs. As a collective group, we can solve any issue that may come our way. But we must stand together and the only way to do that is to stop running our mouths and listen.

Who can you call today and listen to their problems?

March 25th

"If you're born poor, it's not your fault. If you die poor, it is your fault.
-Bill Gates

We all have to start somewhere. But your past doesn't lock you into the future. If you're born without a lot of money, that doesn't mean you can never accumulate it. You have to change your relationship with money if you want it to be part of your life. You must give value to others. If you help others get what they want, you'll get what you want. It's a win-win situation. Money comes to those that know how to use it, save it, invest it, and circulate it wisely. Money goes where it's wanted. If you're always bashing money, you'll never have any. If you take care of it, it will take care of you.

How can you change your relationship with money?

March 26th

"Employ your time in improving yourself by other men's writings so that you shall come easily by what others have labored hard for."
— Socrates

We live in the information age. We are constantly bombarded with social media posts and can look up anything we want to know on the internet. But do we learn anything new from this information? Do we let these words of wisdom from the past sink into our brains and change the way we see the world and how we deal with the problems we face on a daily basis?What about history and ancient writings? Many religious scholars and philosophers study people from the past and how they dealt with stories from the past. The funny thing is, their lives are no different from ours when you set aside technology. They all faced problems with their health, their finances, their relationships, and their careers. Just like us. Can we take the wisdom and know how from their experience and use it to make quantum leaps in ours? Of course! We don't have to reinvent the wheel, as they say. We can learn from the past and use their experience to improve our lives and those of the people that live in our communities. Life is all about improvement and growth and we can do that by learning from others.

What can you learn from someone older?

March 27th

"If you want to find out about the road ahead, then ask about it from those coming back."
-Chinese Proverb

Sometimes you have loved ones that give you advice on subjects they have no experience in. Should you listen to them? Of course not! Would you listen to someone that had lots of debt and was living paycheck to paycheck on how to build wealth? Would you listen to someone that was overweight and never exercised a day in their life on fitness and nutrition? Would you listen to someone that's been divorced twice on how to navigate marriage? Of course not! You can love these people because you know that they're trying to help you, but certainly don't take their advice on anything they have no experience or achievement in. That's heading for disaster and disappointment for sure. Only heed advice from people that live the life you want to live and then implement that advice directly into your daily routines.

What advice are you looking for?

March 28th

"A miracle is really the only way to describe motherhood and giving birth. It's unbelievable how God has made us women and babies to endure and be able to do so much. A miracle indeed. Such an incredible blessing."
-Jennie Finch

Motherhood is one of the most wonderful things any woman can experience. The amount of love that goes into it is unmeasurable and remarkable. For anyone on the fence about having kids or not, think about what it will take from you in order to raise another human being. If you love your life and you don't want to sacrifice your late evening dinners, your size two jeans, and your Friday mani pedi appointments, then you shouldn't have kids. If you want to start a family with someone you truly love and want to spend your time and energy helping the next generation succeed, then you certainly should start a family as soon as possible. Not every woman should have kids. Not every woman is selfless enough to give up something in her life in order to make room for this new person. But for those of us who are lucky and brave enough to make another human, it's one of the most miraculous and wonderful things we could do as women. It's so much fun to be around their personalities and their creativity. It's interesting to see the way they look at the world and their place in it. Being a mom can make you cry, make you laugh, and make you grateful all at the same time. It's truly a wonderful thing to experience.

Show your gratitude for being a mom or having a mom today.

March 29th

"The whole is greater than the sum of its parts."
-Aristotle

Sometimes we think we can do it better by ourselves. And sometimes we're right. Sometimes we think that we shouldn't ask for help because it shows weakness. And sometimes that's right. Sometimes we think that it'll be easier if we do it our way because our way is the only way it should be done. And sometimes it is. But not every situation involves us doing everything by ourselves. Why not work as a team? We can certainly ask our spouse and children to help clean the house. Who cares if the dishes aren't put away properly or they missed some stuff on the floor. At least there's progress, right? Men are a lot better than we are at working with others. They're taught at an early age to work together for the common good. We need to heed this advice. We all have special talents and skills. Why not work together to maneuver the trials of life?Why not ask for help to save time and energy? Nothing needs to be perfect, it just needs to get done. Don't go it alone. Work together with your friends, your family, and your community to better your lives and environment. This can benefit everyone involved.

Who's on your team?

March 30th

"We are more alike, my friends, than we are unalike."

—Maya Angelou, *The Complete Collected Poems of Maya Angelou*

We are all women. We all have the same biological makeup. We all have curves. We all have nurturing souls. We all connect through speech and actions. No matter where you live, no matter how much money you make, or how beautiful your body is, we all come from the same female cloth. We all care about our families. We all love our partners. We all care about our environment and our communities. We all strive to give our children the love and support that only a wonderful mother can provide. No matter what we look like on the outside, no matter where we come from, and no matter where we're going, we're all the same on the inside. Let us band together and help one another lift up the female agenda. Against war, poverty, and suffering. Let us merge our talents and skills into the ultimate female energy that envelopes the entire planet. Only as a collective whole, can we make this planet a world that we want to live in. That's safe and loving for our children to grow up in.

Who can you lend a hand to today and show them support?

March 31st

"I forgive you and set you free. Your actions no longer have power over me. I acknowledge that you are doing the best that you can, and I honor you in your process of unfoldment. You are free and I am free. All is well between us. Peace is the order of the day."

-Michael Bernard Beckwith, *Spiritual Liberation: Fulfilling Your Soul's Potential*

Women in general tend to hold grudges. We hold emotions in. We cry and eat chocolate in the closet because something is affecting us emotionally. We allow others to flood our minds with worry and anxiety. We need to stop this behavior! We are all free creatures with free minds and souls. We have the right to live a free and fulfilling life. In order to do this, we must free our minds of grievances, grudges, and regrets. We must forgive those that have harmed us and not allow other people to control our minds or emotions. When we forgive, we set ourselves free to live the way we want. When we forgive, we release the damaging emotions that upset us and keep us caged. Forgiving doesn't mean forgetting. Forgiving doesn't mean surrendering. What forgiving means is to release the chain that holds us down. Don't we all want to be free of damage that's caused by others? We can't control what others do, but we can control how we respond and feel about a situation. No one can harm you unless you allow them to.

Who can you forgive today and free your mind from your mental torture?

April

Hey Lady,

The weather is changing and the flowers are starting to bloom. It's a great time to do some Spring cleaning! I know, it's not fun, but it needs to get done. When it's not raining, go outside and pick up the sticks and pull weeds. Trim the trees. Clean out the garage and declutter the closets. Look in your closet and find items that you didn't wear this winter. If you didn't wear it, it may be outdated and could be donated for someone else to enjoy. Why not declutter and make some room for new things. What about the kitchen? How many spatulas do you have? Do you need them all? What about the Tupperware containers? Are they missing their lids? If so, get rid of them.

Summer is almost here and would you rather be outside having fun with your friends and family or stuck inside trying to organize all of your crap. Now is a great time to minimize your stuff and keep things tidy and orderly. It will take some work, but will be well worth it in the end. Get your family and spouse or partner on board and pitch stuff!

April 1st

"Better to trip with the feet than with the tongue." -Zeno, founder of Stoicism.

Have you ever said something terrible to someone and regretted it? Of course, everyone has. What Zeno was saying is that we can trip over something physical and recover from it, but if we say something to someone, we may not be able to fix the relationship. Words hurt. Words can cause strong emotions. Men fight wars over words. Women destroy relationships over words. Words matter. Some people are more susceptible to the emotions that can be tied to specific words. Others can control their emotions no matter what words are used. You never know how someone will react to words and phrases so it's best to take a moment and think about what words you are going to say *before* you say them. Respond intelligently rather than reacting emotionally.

Will you think twice before speaking up today?

April 2nd

"A day without laughter is a day wasted."
-Nicolas Chamfort

Life is too short to not have fun. Live life like children. They see the world with curiosity and imagination. They draw on instinct and creativity when they play. Why can't we do the same? As we get older, our time is ruled by obligation. We work, we take care of the house, we take care of the kids, we give to our spouses and communities. It's no wonder we burn out. It's no wonder we're tired and frustrated. We need to stop the madness and carve out some time to have some fun. Be silly. Draw, dance, and drink. We need to be grateful for what we have and imagine the things we want and have a little fun while doing it.

What would a day look like for you that consists of nothing but fun?

April 3rd

"Surround yourself only with people who are going to take you higher."
-Oprah Winfrey

Are there people in your life that you don't particularly like? That you don't agree with? That you can't wait to get away from? Do these people even contribute to your life in any way? Then why are you still hanging around them? Why are they even a fixture in your life? Whether they are a close "friend" or a family member, you're under no obligation to continue having a relationship with that person. Especially if they're not doing anything positive for you. Can you really talk with this person? Can you really trust this person? Then why are you continuing to be around them? Life's too short to be miserable. Life's too short to not be around people that love you, support you, and have fun with you. Improve your peer group and they will raise you to their level. Network with people that are living a life that you desire. That has what you want. That exudes the characteristics that you desire. Declutter the deadbeats in your life and you'll find a heavy weight has been lifted off your shoulders.

Who needs to be eliminated from your friend circle?

April 4th

"Strong minds discuss ideas, average minds discuss events, weak minds discuss people."
- Socrates

Do you gossip? Do you have an opinion about everything that happens? Why not rise above the chatter? Talking about ideas helps to improve our civilization. Talking about other people nevers changes anything. People don't change much. Women tend to complain about things that are out of their control. This idle chatter never does anything good. It keeps you in a state of disappointment and frustration which gets you nowhere fast. Why put yourself in that position? Start thinking about what you can control and improve upon and stop complaining and bitching about things that you can't.

What ideas do you have that can start to help others?

April 5th

"Never underestimate the power you have to take your life in a new direction."
- Germany Kent

You're a woman. You're strong. You've survived several crises over the years. You grab ahold of the day and spit it out like it's a piece of gum. You do what's asked of you without question. You go to sleep and get up the next day to do it all again. But what if this life that you created doesn't satisfy you anymore? What if you want to make a change? Are you scared to make a change? Are you crippled without the knowledge on how to do it? Change is very difficult for people to make. It requires us to get out of our safety zone and try something new. But isn't that what life is about? Really living life requires us to get out of our safety zone. To jump and fall. To get back up and jump again. It's trial and tribulation. It's conquest and victory. It's using our curiosity and ambition to get us out of bed and eager to start the new day. It's the courage to take your life in a new direction. Don't be scared. Be excited that today you'll start something new!

What new adventure can you start today?

April 6th

"One morning you wake up with more life behind you than in front of you, not being able to understand how it's happened."
-Fredrik Backman, *Britt-Marie var här*

Mid life is around the corner for all of us. One day you'll wake up and realize that your time on this Earth is limited. You look in the mirror and notice your skin is starting to wrinkle. You get out of bed in the morning and your body starts cracking in places you didn't realize you had. You're tired after a long day at work. You're not as enthusiastic about your day as you once were. Welcome to middle age. If you're not there yet, this is what's in store for you. If you're there, you already know what I'm talking about. If you're past it, congrats, you survived long enough to get older. No matter what stage you're in, take some time and reflect on what you've accomplished in your life, where you are currently, and dream of where you want to go. Make some goals to strive for. Make some plans you want to pursue. Travel. Learn something new. Start a hobby. Enjoy your life, because this is it ladies. Today is the only day that's guaranteed to occur.

Today is a great time to think about the future. What goals/plans do you want to pursue?

April 7th

"Returning home is the most difficult part of long-distance hiking; You have grown outside the puzzle and your piece no longer fits."
-Cindy Ross

Once you've accomplished a goal, there's no turning back to the beginning. You've grown and you're not the same person as you were when you first started. You act differently. You think differently and you get different results. This is who you are now. There's no turning back. There's no returning home. Maybe you're sad because you're outgrowing your old girlfriends. Maybe you're lonely because your dreams aren't the same as your loved ones. No one said you couldn't reach for your dreams and goals. You may need to look for other people as your support net who have the same wants and goals. There's one thing for sure in life, it's nice to go back home to visit, but you'd never want to live there again.

What/who must you give up in order to manifest your dreams and goals?

April 8th

"If anyone on the verge of action should judge himself according to the outcome, he would never begin."
- Søren Kierkegaard, *Fear and Trembling*

Never be afraid of failing. You're learning something new today and of course you won't be an expert at it in the beginning. That's okay. No one expects you to be. You deserve to make a change and you've finally decided to take the first step. Sometimes that step will be easy, and sometimes there's a lot of consequences that go along with it. Who cares? You're finally changing something! You're finally moving. You're finally taking that job you've always wanted to take. You're finally meeting that special someone. You're finally taking a chance on yourself. Never sell yourself short for the courage you're displaying. Never doubt yourself. You've got this girl! You can do anything you want. You can have anything you want. Take a deep breath and jump in. You may get a little beat up. That's okay, you'll heal and be stronger for it. You may need to learn something new, that's okay, the knowledge is there for you to learn. No matter what, don't stop. Live the life of your dreams and don't allow anyone or anything to get in your way.

What's been holding you back from living the life you want?

April 9th

"Commitment to a proposition with a truth condition is belief, and call any other kind of commitment a stance."
-Simon Blackburn, *Content and Truth*

Do we really have to drive around the state to drop off our kids at travel soccer? Must we volunteer at school because all of the other moms are doing it? Do we really believe that we're not good enough to get the promotion over Bob because he's part of the boys' club? What are we telling ourselves? Are they beliefs that are factual and true, or are they opinions and stances that direct our actions? Be very careful to live on opinions and stances alone.

What things are you truly committed to? What things can you give up that are getting in the way of your happiness and true self?

April 10th

"Above all, it is necessary for a person to have a true self estimate, for we commonly think we can do more than we really can."
-Seneca, On Tranquility of Mind, 5.2.

Most of us try to be super women! We go to work, we run our kids to soccer practice. We cook and we clean. We are tigresses in the bedroom. We do this day in and day out. Everyday the same thing. It's no wonder we feel stressed and burnt out. We often think we can "do it all" but in reality, no one expects us to. It's all in our own heads. We need to give ourselves a break. We need to take some time for ourselves every day and relax a little. The laundry can wait. Someone else can take your kid to practice. It's okay to say no to things. You don't have to do it all. You don't have to sacrifice your time and energy for everyone else. It's okay to not be superwoman! It's okay to have some free time to do what you want to do for a change. If everyone else gets your time and energy, why not give yourself the same luxury? You deserve to work on your own mental and physical health. To assess where you are in your journey of life and to have some space to explore new options and opportunities.

What things can you eliminate in your schedule today?

April 11th

"Few tasks are more like the torture of Sisyphus than housework, with its endless repetition: the clean becomes soiled, the soiled is made clean, over and over, day after day."

-Simone de Beauvoir, *The Second Sex*

Most women take on the house cleaning. There's always chores to be done. Sweeping and mopping. Dusting. Wiping. Laundry. Dishes. It's never ending. An easy way to keep up with it is to do a little every day. What's the main areas of the house that get the most use? Kitchen and living room. Make those a daily priority. If you can keep them decluttered and swept, that's most of your battle. Consider keeping appliances in cabinets instead of on the counters and all you have to do is wipe the cleared counters every day. Keep the toys and remotes in their own spots and keep end tables and coffee tables clear of clutter. Do a general pick up before bed and your main rooms will look clean and fresh for the next day. If you need help, consider a cleaning service. Even if it's once a month- let them do the deep cleaning for you and keep your home fresh and clean without spending your time and energy doing it yourself.

What chores must I do today? What chores can I delegate?

April 12th

"Of all the means to insure happiness throughout the whole life, by far the most important is the acquisition of friends."
- Epicurus, *A Guide To Happiness*

Who are your girlfriends? Who are the ladies you love to hang out with? Who are the people that always listen and lend you a helping hand when you need one? These ladies are your tribe. These ladies are your friends that you'll live your life with. Treasure them. Spend as much time with them. Listen to them. Realize that there's not a lot of things on Earth more precious than your friendships. These friendships need to be nurtured and not neglected. These women need to know how important they are to you. Tell them. Share with them. Let them feel the love that you have for them. Let go of the ones that take you for granted. Let go of the ones that are never around when you really need them. Let go of the ones that never call you back. You don't need these people. You need the ones that want to spend time with you and that listen and help you. They are your true friends. Celebrate your friendships every time you get together.

Today's assignment: Make plans with your best girlfriend and let her know how much she means to you.

April 13th

"I'm as flawed as the next person. But maybe I inspire women because I'm an example that you should never assume that where you are in life or what you're doing is going to remain exactly as it is forever."
-Ree Drummond

Change is inevitable. We grow and improve. We can attract new people and opportunities into our lives. We can rest assured knowing that tomorrow is a new day with new beginnings. Embrace where you are now, knowing that it can always change for the better. Jump through the necessary hoops to make it happen. Learn the skills that can skyrocket your success. Network with people that have the lives you want to live. Listen to them and take the actions they tell you to take. Then and only then can you see your circumstances change and improve.

What changes do you want to make?

April 14th

"Who is Invincible? The one who cannot be upset by anything outside their reasoned choice."
-Epictetus

Women are emotional creatures. No one can deny that. It's good to get out our feelings and frustrations sometimes. But when we do this on a continuous basis, we make ourselves vulnerable to the world around us. People learn that they can control and manipulate us. This manipulation oftentimes satisfies *their* agendas and does nothing to satisfy *ours.* Can we take a moment and step back from the situation before our emotions consume us and control our reactions? Yes. Can we decide that we don't need to form an opinion about the subject matter that's before us? Yes. Is it okay that we take our time in making a decision so we can look at both sides of the coin so we don't make a mistake? Yes. Commenting and making decisions rationally instead of emotionally is an important path to leading a happy and satisfying life. No one wins on emotional decisions.

Can you avoid getting upset today?

April 15th

"Experience is the teacher of all things."
-Julius Caesar

In order for us to gain experience, we must take a chance. A risk. To venture out of our safety zone and try something new. And fail miserably at it. And to try again in order to figure it out. That's the only way to gain experience. You've got to do something new. Something different. And not be afraid to try and fail. No one is great at first. It takes time and a lot of practice to be great at something. You'll learn what to avoid and what to embrace. You'll learn who can help you and who can't. You'll learn how to treat other people and how you want to be treated. Life will give you lemons and you can decide whether you can make lemonade from them or not. Live your life to the fullest and experience all that it has to offer.

What can you experience today?

April 16th

"Make today worth remembering."
- Zig Ziglar

We often get caught up in mundane tasks. Sometimes we find ourselves at the end of the day and wonder where our day went. Sometimes we spend our time doing things that don't matter. Why waste our lives like that? Today is a great day to do something new or something fun. Today is a great day to plan a great experience and create adventure. Why wait? Tomorrow isn't certain for any of us. Tomorrow is out of our control. But today is ready for us to make the most of it. Today is the only thing that's certain. Do something different. Do something fun. Be silly. Make memories with the ones you love.

How are you going to make today memorable?

April 17th

"Everything is hard before it is easy."
-Johann Wolfgang von Goethe

No one begins as a master. No one gets the right answer at first. It takes time for us to learn a new skill. It takes time for us to improve and become better. Sometimes we need better teachers. Sometimes we need to invest more time and energy. But if we keep learning and improving, we can become experts at anything. Being patient and willing to fail is the only way that success is assured. Taking each step, improving to each level is a direct path to becoming a master. Humility and openness rewards those that pursue their ambitions.

What's the next step today?

April 18th

"People in general would rather die than forgive. It's *that* hard. If God said in plain language. "I'm giving you a choice, forgive or die," a lot of people would go ahead and order their coffin."
-Sue Monk Kidd

It can be difficult to admit when you're wrong. It can be difficult to ask for forgiveness. It can be even harder to forgive someone else who has wronged you. We're all humans and we all make mistakes. But their mistakes should not define who they really are. Sometimes they're going through a rough patch of their lives. Sometimes they struggle to do what's right. Sometimes they need love and support. Rather than giving up and cutting them off, we need to find our inner strength, give forgiveness for not being their best self, and decide to help them move in another direction. When we do this, they will find the love and support they need to make the changes and correct the wrongs they've done. We need to forgive them and give them the grace that can give everyone hope for a better tomorrow.

Is there someone you can forgive today?

April 19th

"It's the days you have every right to break down and fall apart, yet choose to show up anyway that matters most. Don't diminish the small steps that others can't see."
-Brittany Burgunder

Some days you'd rather stay in bed than work out. Some days you really don't want to deal with the kids. Some days are more difficult than others. This is life. But in order to control the day, you must show up. You must put in the hard work to get the results you want. You must push and struggle a little in order to persevere. That's how it goes. Some days will be filled with happiness and ease while others can be tedious. It's the tedious days that make you stronger. It's the tedious days that you learn the most. It's the tedious days that will propel you to a higher standard. Embrace the hard days and know that no matter what happens, you showed up and you gave it your best.

Will you show up today?

April 20th

"Learn everything you can, anytime you can, from anyone you can, there will always come a time when you will be grateful you did."
- Sarah Caldwel

Everyone has something to give to the world. We must open our minds to learning new things every day. There are thousands of new ideas floating out there for us to build upon. Is there something we can improve? Is there someone we can help? Is there a problem we can solve? Look and ye shall find. In order to grow and improve, we must learn new things about us and the world we live in. We must change our thinking and our beliefs about our limitations. Anything is possible if we believe it is. If we want to grow, we must be willing to put our egos aside and implement what our mentors are trying to teach us.

What can you learn today?

April 21st

"Time crumbles things; everything grows old under the power of Time and is forgotten through the lapse of Time."
-Aristotle

Like it or not, time waits for no one. Time is our most precious resource yet most of us waste a lot of it worrying and doing things we don't want to do. We must wake up and realize how precious and valuable our time really is! We must organize our time and prioritize how we spend it. We must focus our attention only on things that matter to us. We must spend our time doing things we love with the people we love. We must get rid of distractions and interruptions and attend to matters that move us one step towards our goals and dreams. We must take the time to relax and re-energize. We must spend some time every day reflecting on what's working and what's not working in our life. When we focus on what we want and enjoy the fruits of our labor, we'll indeed feel happy.

How are you spending your time today?

April 22nd

"The man who does more than he is paid for will soon be paid for more than he does."
- Napoleon Hill

The secret to making more money is giving more value. This means that if you help more people get what they want and to solve their problems with your products and services, they'll compensate you with money. Thus, everyone gets what they want. They get what they want, and you get what you want. Sometimes we must stay late at work and our kids will have to wait. Sometimes we'll have to correct a mistake that someone else makes. Sometimes we'll have to spend our own money to help someone out. This is called customer service. This is called going above and beyond. This is called being successful. When you think about your customer's needs more than your own, money will reward you for your time and effort. If it doesn't, you'll need to go where your time and effort is appreciated.

What can you do to help your customer today?

April 23rd

"Do not read, as children do, to amuse yourself, or like the ambitious, for the purpose of instruction. No, read in order to live."
-Gustave Flaubert

There is so much knowledge and practical advice stored in books. Some of us read books in order to escape from our daily routines. Some of us read books to gain new skills that can help us achieve our goals. Some of us read books to better understand ourselves. All of these purposes are valid and can serve us well. Philosophy can be read to help us live our best life. Philosophy is meant to question the reasoning behind the way we think about things and about how we act in certain situations. We can use all of the knowledge found in books to improve our lives. We can implement these ideas and create a life that we don't need a vacation from. We can learn how to live a life of meaning and purpose. We can fill our lives with people we love and with the things that can make a difference. We can strengthen our weaknesses and open our minds to new and exciting adventures. When we read books and implement the ideas into our own lives, we can alter our fate and the fates of our families. And you can do all of this for free at your local library!

What do you want to learn? What book do you want to start reading today?

April 24th

"Teachers open the door. You enter by yourself."
-Chinese Proverb

There's information everywhere. Whether it's good or not has yet to be seen. But are you ready to learn something? That's the question. When you open your mind to new ideas, thoughts, and possibilities, you open your mind to the world. Prior experiences. Philosophy on different ways to think and live your life. DIY how to videos. Fictional stories. History. All of these ideas have been captured in books, audio, and video. Are you willing to change your beliefs and limitations in order to grow and improve your life? Are you willing to be humble and learn from someone who is more successful than you? Are you willing to change? If so, there's a plethora of information for you to absorb and implement in your own life. Much of this information is free for you to use. YouTube and your local library house millions of ideas and concepts just waiting for you to explore. Start learning new skills that can make you more money in your career, new hobbies that can improve your mental and physical shape, and new ideas that can make you an overall better and more generous person.

What's something new that you can learn today?

April 25th

"A woman has to live her life, or live to repent not having lived it."
- D.H. Lawrence, *Lady Chatterley's Lover*

Do you ever think of death? It's not a great topic to wake up to today, but it's a very important subject to help motivate you to live your life to the fullest. The average age of a woman's life is 75 years. That's only 3900 weeks. That's only 27,300 days. Where are you in your life journey? How much time do you have left? When you're young and carefree, you never think about wasting time. But as you age and your time is spent checking things off your list, you realize that time is precious and also goes by fast. You see how fast your children grow up. You see how fast your hair turns gray and the wrinkles set in and you realize that time waits for no one. The question you should ask yourself today is, "Have you done everything you've wanted to do?" Have you traveled where you want to visit yet? Are you the person you want to be? Do you have the amount of money you want? Is your house the way you want it? Do you have the memories you want to have with your family and friends? If not, it's time to start doing all of the things you want to do. Tomorrow is never guaranteed. Today is the day to live your life on your terms with no regrets and no limitations.

Have you done everything you've wanted to do? What's still on the list?

April 26th

"The more you struggle to live, the less you live. Give up the notion that you must be sure of what you are doing. Instead, surrender to what is real within you, for that alone is sure. You are above everything distressing."
- Spinoza

Most women love to be safe and secure. We can be very calculating and hesitant. We don't like to make mistakes and we certainly don't want to feel vulnerable. So sometimes we don't act. Sometimes we sit on the sidelines and wait for someone else to act or to see what the outcome is. What we need to realize is that in order for us to improve and grow, we need to make changes. We need to take risks and to fail and learn as we go. We can still be safe and calculating, but at some time, we must take the first step in order to live the life we really want. Struggling and suffering is not what God wants us to experience. We can't be happy if we're always filled with fear. We must realize that we're strong enough to tackle anything that comes our way because we are women. When we trust ourselves and our instincts, we can allow ourselves to venture out of our comfort zones and into the adventure that awaits us. Aren't you relieved that you're capable and worthy of success? There's nothing your instincts can do to lead you in the wrong direction. Listen to them and let them guide you to the life you want to live.

Your instincts are talking to you today. What are they telling you to do?

April 27th

"One must wait until the evening to see how splendid the day has been."
-Sophocles

It's important to reflect on the day. How do we know if we were productive and taking steps towards our goals if we don't track our progress? Writing down our goals is important, but tracking our progress on our goals is critical in achieving them. How do we know how close we are to achieving our goal unless we measure it? How do we know if we need to pivot or do more if we don't keep track? How do we know if our goals still wake us up in the morning unless we revisit them daily? Checking off the things on our 'To Do' List only works if those things are directly tied to our goals. If it's just *busy* work that's being done, it won't count because it's not moving the needle towards our goal achievement. Reflecting on our day and planning our next move for tomorrow is the key to taking the next steps towards living the life we truly want to live.

How did your day go today? Did you move towards your goal?

April 28th

"To exist is to change, to change is to mature, to mature is to go on creating oneself endlessly."
-Henri Bergson

When we're young, we think we know it all. Then we move out and start our life on our own and realize there's more to life than our parents' house. When we start living on our own, the world starts to open up to us. We're flooded with new ideas and new ways of living. Then we hit our 30s and start to become set in our ways. We settle. We compromise. We allow our comfort zone to take a strong hold on our thoughts, beliefs, and actions. We become complacent. That doesn't sound exciting, does it? If we want to do something new, there's nothing stopping us but our own habits. If we change our habits, we can change the actions needed to accomplish the goal we want. We can constantly learn and apply new ideas and actions into our lives, thus improving it on a measurable scale. We don't need permission to make a change. We need courage to make the change. We need persistence and a clear vision on what we want the outcome to be. Then we can recreate ourselves continuously and live extraordinary lives. Doesn't that sound exciting?

What changes do you want to make today?

April 29th

"All you need is love. But a little chocolate now and then doesn't hurt."
-Charles M. Schulz

Today's going to be a busy day. You've got a lot on your plate. Today's quote reminds us all that we need to treat ourselves every once in a while. It's okay to lock the kids out, draw a bubble bath, and drink a glass of wine while listening to your favorite 90s music. It's okay to stop by your favorite restaurant for some take out. It's okay to go to the store and grab some of your favorite truffles. It's okay if you want to share your favorite things with your friends and loved ones, but it's also okay to keep them for yourself. It's okay to be selfish. It's okay to do the things you love. It's okay to relax and re-energize. Everyone needs downtime. Everyone needs to participate in their favorite activity or hobby. Everyone deserves a break from the everyday hustle. Use today to remind yourself that you're working hard and that you deserve a break.

What can you do today to reward yourself?

April 30th

"Beauty is only skin deep, but ugly goes clean to the bone."
- Dorothy Parker

Have you ever met someone that's beautiful on the outside but once you got to know her, she was ugly as sin on the inside? Many women are praised for their outside beauty and never work on being a good person. Being kind. Being thoughtful. Being helpful. These women tend to be selfish and self-absorbed. These are people that are very shallow and will cut you deep if given the opportunity. My advice? Stay away from them. They're not worth it. They will either drag you into the darkness with them or they will cut you loose before you have a chance to blink. Make sure you're not only beautiful on the outside, but that you're equally beautiful on the inside. There's a lot to be said for inner beauty.

How can you show your inner beauty today?

May

Hey Lady,

May is a special time of year when we celebrate our mothers. We should break out the old photos of us and our siblings when we were kids and remember the good ol' days. Call your mom and tell her you love her. Facetime with her and let her see your smiling face. That's all she wants from you, right?

If you're a mom, spend some time with your kids. They need your love and support. Ask them how they are and what's new in their lives. Are they in love? Are they in the middle of an important project? Have they eaten a good meal lately? Maybe it's time to invite them over and cook them their favorite food. It's amazing how a home cooked meal warms your heart and brings you close.

Rekindle ties with your family this month and feel the love they have for you.

May 1st

"You are not your body and hairstyle, but your capacity for choosing well. If your choices are beautiful, so too will you be."
-Epictetus from *Discourses 3.1.39b-40a.*

Women's bodies and beauty are put on a pedestal. The problem is, as we age, our beauty ages and isn't valued as it once was. For some, this can be devastating. For others, it's a wakeup call that you aren't your body. Your beauty comes from within. Make good choices. Live a great life. Love people who are worthy of your love. When you're kind, loving, and helpful to others, your beauty will radiate for everyone to see regardless of your physical beauty.

What will you do today to show the world how beautiful you are on the outside?

May 2nd

"Do you want to know what you think about most of the time? Take a look at the results you're getting. That will tell you exactly what's going on inside."
-Bob Proctor

Our thoughts create our realities. If we want something, we can think about it, find out how to get it, and then follow the actions steps to get it. But what do you think about daily? Do you have worry, fear, or anxiety? Are you always negative thinking that things won't turn out for you or work in your favor? If you're negative, The Universe will give you more of what you're thinking about. If you're grateful and thankful for what you have right now, The Universe will look out for you and give you happiness because you will always show gratitude for what you have. Our realities are created by our thoughts and beliefs about the world and how we live in it. If we think that we'll never get ahead, we won't do what it takes to jump the curb. If we don't feel beautiful on the inside, no one will be attracted to us no matter what our bodies look like. We all have a sense of attraction for one another. Some people exude happiness, positivity, and love. While others exude the opposite. Who do you want to be around? Someone who's optimistic, positive, and ambitious? Or someone that plays the victim and blames everyone else for their problems?

If your reality is directly tied to your thoughts, what are three positive thoughts you can have right now that can help you live the life you deserve?

May 3rd

"Each person deserves a day away in which no problems are confronted, no solutions searched for."

—Maya Angelou, *Wouldn't Take Nothing for My Journey Now*

Women love to multitask. To act like superwoman. To do everything that is asked so as not to disappoint. But in the end, everyone gets what they want and leaves us exhausted and run down. Every woman needs a break. A break from being a mom. A break from being the boss. A break from being a wife. A break from being a project leader. Maybe it's time for a weekend away. Maybe it's time for a simple hot bubble bath. Maybe it's time for a delicious meal that someone else cooks and cleans up. We all need a break and we need it now. Make plans this weekend for a little time alone to recharge your battery so you can be ready to go on Monday morning. If you can't get away for the weekend, make an appointment at your local spa for a massage or a facial. Just a little something that makes you feel relaxed, pampered, and appreciated. Do something for yourself for a change and don't make an excuse for it. You deserve it!

What are you going to do to pamper yourself this week?

May 4th

"One is not born, but, rather, becomes a woman."

-Simone de Beauvoir, *The Second Sex*

Being a woman doesn't come from certain biological entities or psychology but by the differences that occur in our civilization. We are not born women. We are born as girls who grow up and take on the societal norms of womanhood. We play a role as determined by men and culture. At least that's what some people think. What do you think? Is there a preconceived notion in society about women? Why do we tell our sons to "Stop being a pussy?" Do we not realize that a women's biological system is far more complicated and superior than men's? We tend to look down on being a woman because we lack the physical strength of a man. But in reality, we are far superior with the ability to produce life and nurture the world with our love.

How will you celebrate being a woman today?

May 5th

"There is a lie that acts like a virus within the mind of humanity. And that lie is, 'There's not enough good to go around. There's lack and there's limitation and there's just not enough.The truth is that there's more than enough good to go around. There are more than enough creative ideas. There is more than enough power. There is more than enough love. There's more than enough joy. All of this begins to come through a mind that is aware of its own infinite nature.There is enough for everyone. If you believe it, if you can see it, if you act from it, it will show up for you. That's the truth."

-Michael Beckwith

How many women doubt themselves? How many women think they're not strong enough, smart enough, or pretty enough? We often compare ourselves negatively to others, thinking we don't have enough of what's required to live the life of our dreams. But this is a false belief that someone put in our brains that stuck with us throughout our adolescence and adulthood. Every woman deserves happiness. Every woman deserves to feel confidence in herself and her abilities. Every woman must believe that The Universe will provide just what she needs. Mother Nature always provides. She never disappoints. Believe in yourself and your abilities. You got this! You're a wonderful woman! You're beautiful. You're intelligent. You're creative. You're remarkable and have so much to offer the world. Now it's your turn to show them what you have. Are you ready? Let's go!

What lies are you going to get rid of that kill your confidence and worthiness?

May 6th

"Happiness depends upon ourselves."
-Aristotle

We often look for happiness when something happens. Or when we finish something. Or when we meet someone. Or when someone does something. "I will be happy when..." Instead of waiting for happiness after someone or something happens to cross our path, why not be happy with our lives as they are right now? Why not be happy that you're alive and you have the freedom to make the day the way you want? Why do we look to a certain result or outcome in order for us to be satisfied with our effort? It doesn't have to be that way. We can look around and realize that nothing will cause us satisfaction.

What can you be happy about today that has nothing to do with anyone or anything else? Can you be happy just because?

May 7th

"Do one thing every day that scares you."
–Eleanor Roosevelt, *You Learn by Living*

We live in our comfort zones. In our routines. By our daily habits. When we stay in our safe zone, we continue to get the same results. Day after day. Week after week. Month after month. Year after year. And sometimes that's great. We're healthy, we're wealthy, and we've got great relationships. But what if we're out of shape? What if we don't have two nickels to rub together? What if we have lousy relationships or worst yet, none at all? How do we get out of our rut and start living the life we want and deserve? It all starts with us. It all starts with learning how to get in shape. Diet. Exercise. It starts by learning about money and how to make more and invest it. We must network with new people and surround ourselves with new ideas that can improve our skills and natural talents. By getting out of our safe, reliable comfort zones, we can be, do, and have anything we want. But it will be scary at times. It will be nerve-racking. It will take time, energy, and perseverance in order to manifest the results we're after. But who cares? You're doing it for you. You're not doing it for anyone else, and as long as you're okay with your results, that's the only person that matters!

What do you need to improve?

May 8th

"Whatever you are looking for is also looking for you. You see, don't only look. Be available and ready when it shows up."
-Sahndra Fon Dufe

We live in a dynamic, ever-changing Universe. Every imaginable scenario is available and waiting to manifest. Every decision we make has consequences. Every decision we make changes our future path. We are constantly faced with chances to grow and improve our lives. Do we hesitate to make those changes? Do we hesitate to step out of our comfort zones? Many women fear the unknown. We love certainty and safety. But our future self is waiting for us to mature into her. She's waiting for us to make the right decisions and improve ourselves in order to live our best lives. What are you waiting for?

What do you want your future to look like?

May 9th

"Whether you think you can or whether you think you can't, you're right."
-Henry Ford

Our thoughts create the actions we take. Our actions then give us the results we experience. Over time, those thoughts can become beliefs. Over time, our actions become precedent for what results we can expect. If we think we can't get the result we're after because we've tried in the past and it never turned out the way we wanted, we may not take the opportunity again when it presents itself. Past performance should never hinder trying again. You'll never succeed if you give up after you fall. Failure is another step towards success. It will take many obstacles and fumbles in order to learn what you must do correctly to meet your goals. If you doubt your success from the start, you will close any chance of succeeding in the future. It all starts with your thoughts and beliefs.

What goal do you think you can accomplish?

May 10th

"Failing to plan is planning to fail."
-Benjamin Franklin

Every accomplishment needs a set plan. A roadmap. A blueprint. We need a blueprint in order to build a house. We need a flight plan in order to land at JFK. We need a financial plan in order to retire with financial independence. We need to plan our parenting style with our spouse in order to be consistent with our children. We need a recipe if we're going to bake a cake. All goals need a path that's mapped out and followed. Without a plan, we are aimlessly roaming around. Without a plan, we have no intention with our resources. Without a plan, we can't succeed.

What is your plan for your next goal?

May 11th

"Spend extravagantly on the things you love, and cut costs mercilessly on the things you don't.

-Ramit Sethi, *I Will Teach You to Be Rich*

In order to live a financially stressless life, we must live within our means. This means we must be frugal. But this doesn't mean that we can't have fun and enjoy our favorite things. Quite the contrary. Being frugal and living within our means, means that we can have anything we want, but we can't have everything we want all at once. We must prioritize our money. If we love our Starbucks, but don't care about expensive shoes, then our money should be spent on daily Starbucks and not buying expensive shoes, even if they're on sale. If we love to travel but don't care how big our house is, we should spend our money on taking fun trips around the world and not worry about the square footage of our house. Prioritizing our money can help us enjoy it without causing anxiety about the amount. You can be wealthy and never have the time to enjoy your wealth, or you can be middle class, and have the best time ever without a care in the world.

What does your financial world look like?

May 12th

"Midlife: when the Universe grabs your shoulders and tells you "I'm not f-ing around, use the gifts you were given."
-Brene Brown

Everyone has talents. Some people can draw. Some people can sing. Some people are good with numbers. Some people are good communicators. Some people can cook. What are your talents? Is your career aligned with your inner skills? Are there things you love to do? Are there things you're good at? Those are the things you should pursue. Our lives are finite. We don't know how long we will live. Why waste time doing things we don't love? Why waste time being around people that don't enrich our lives? Simply, why waste time? Today is a great day to start living your best life. Don't live in regret. Start today.

What do you love to do?

May 13th

"I didn't get there by wishing for it or hoping for it, but by working for it."
- Estée Lauder

Some people think that the rich are greedy bastards. And some are. Other people think that they are entitled to certain perks just because they are breathing. But most aren't. If you talk with any successful person, you will realize that 99% of them worked for their success. And they worked hard for it. They endured countless obstacles and criticism. They spent thousands and thousands of hours trying and failing their way to success. They spent tons of money, some of which they didn't have and had to borrow, to realize their dream. But there's one thing they did, that unsuccessful people don't do. They didn't quit. They kept moving forward. No matter what happened or what they were told, they kept moving towards their dreams. You can be successful and live the way you want to live, no matter what scale that is. But it won't be easy and it won't be given to you. In order to cross the finish line, you've got to run the race!

What are you working for today?

May 14th

"Prefer knowledge to wealth, for the one is transitory, the other perpetual."
-Socrates

Money comes and goes, but knowledge and wisdom can last forever. It can be passed to other people and from generation to generation. Once we had the written word, we used that luxury to help the future generations springboard to newer ideas and concepts. Our society became better. Our health improved. Our wealth increased. Technology soared. If you use ideas and concepts from those that are successful, you too can obtain success. With success comes wealth and prosperity that can be passed throughout your family, friends, and communities. But wealth can dissipate. Knowledge exists forever. Whether you use that knowledge is completely up to you. You don't have to reinvent the wheel. You can use the knowledge and experience from past generations and use it to improve your life and those around you. Improving old ideas is how innovation exists. Linking and expanding old concepts helps to expand our awareness of what is possible. And that's what helps to shift cultures, society, and build new modern beliefs.

What can you learn today?

May 15th

"Either you run the day or the day runs you."
- Jim Rohn

It's not difficult to let the day get away from us. Sometimes we find ourselves doing chores all day or sitting around watching Netflix. But these things help us move any closer to our goals. Our goals are never on vacation. They never take the night or the weekends off and neither should we. It's okay to have some relaxation time, but we can relax after we've done something towards our goals. Right down one thing you can accomplish in the next hour that can get you closer to hitting your target. It could be an extra sales call to someone new. It could be eating the salad instead of the burger. It could be creating a budget spreadsheet and actually filling it out. Take the next step towards success. You'll be glad you did!

How are you controlling today?

May 16th

"Create. Not for the money. Not for the fame. Not for the recognition. But for the pure joy of creating something and sharing it."
-Ernest Barbaric

Do you love to paint? Or cook? Or crochet? Or sing? Everyone has a skill and talent they not only enjoy but are good at. These skills and talents should be shared with the world. Not because you'll become a professional, but because you need to release them. You need to have fun in life. You need to show others what you can do. You're good and others should acknowledge it. Be proud of your talents and hobbies. Dive deeper into them and spend your free time getting better at them. You only go around once, so why not enjoy the things you're good at? Be creative and explore all your thoughts and intuitions. You never know what can come from it.

What can you create today?

May 17th

"What you do makes a difference, and you have to decide what kind of difference you want to make."
-Jane Goodall

There are global problems. There are community problems. There are problems with the economy. There are family problems. There are health concerns. There are difficult family dynamics to address. No one can deny the negative in the world. But we all can make a difference. Big and small. The great thing about these problems is that we all can contribute our skills and talents to their resolve. We can spend our money and time to help our families and our communities. No one's part is too small or not enough. The effort brought together compounds tremendously over time. One community can bring forth a major change that can help all of its citizens. One person can help organize a fundraiser that can help a family member receive medical care that they would not otherwise afford. When our hearts are big, and our efforts follow, any problems can be overcome. It takes vision and a charitable soul to help make a difference.

What charity can you contribute to today?

May 18th

"If you can remember why you started, then you will know why you must continue."
- Chris Burkmenn

It's never easy to go after a goal. You're chartering new territory and often stumble. It takes a lot of time and energy to figure things out. Sometimes your mentor stears you in the wrong direction and you must start again. Sometimes you find that the goal you're going after changes and you must pivot your path. There's always going to be a gestation period of obtaining your goals. Sometimes the goals are so big that it can take a lifetime to achieve them. It's easier to achieve your goals if you cut them down into more obtainable, bite-size chunks that you can achieve quicker and easier. No one said you had to hit them today. But if you can take another step towards them, then you've conquered your day. Know why you want to achieve the goal and your why will push you through any obstacle that finds you.

What is your reason why?

May 19th

"Maybe I made a mistake yesterday, but yesterday's me is still me. I am who I am today, with all my faults. Tomorrow I might be a tiny bit wiser, and that's me, too. These faults and mistakes are what I am, making up the brightest stars in the constellation of my life. I have come to love myself for who I was, who I am, and who I hope to become."
- Kim Namjoong

Our mistakes don't define us. We're human and we're doing the best we can to navigate through life. All of us are met with different adversities. All of us have different temperaments and goals. That's what makes us unique and wonderful. We have the luxury of failing, learning, and taking a different course of action. We can dream and follow our dreams. We must love and accept all of our strengths and weaknesses. That's what makes us feel alive and full of the divine. Always be progressing. Always be improving. Never settle for anything but the best. Always know that you're loved and you're enough in this world no matter what happens.

Have you made a mistake? Can you get past it?

May 20th

"You can only work on yourself. Start there."
- Alice O. Howell

The only person I'm in charge of is me. I can't do anything to change you. I can try to convince you or help you change, but the only one that can change you is you. That should free you from worry. That should free you from anxiety. You can relax and know that the only thing you have to control is you. Let the chips fall as they may. You can play the game any way you see fit. You can accomplish any goal you set your mind to. As long as you're responsible for the thoughts you're thinking, the feelings you're feeling, and the actions you're taking, that's all you can do. The results will happen the way you want them to as long as you're taking the appropriate actions and visualizing the end of the journey. Control what you can control and leave the rest to God and the Universe to deal with. Don't worry about how you're going to do it, the steps will be shown if you put yourself in the right position.

What are you going to work on today?

May 21st

"One must always be prepared for riotous and endless waves of transformation."
- Elizabeth Gilbert, *Eat, Pray, Love*

Every day we wake up with the opportunity to make a change. Every day presents itself with a different opportunity that we can explore. Every day is a new beginning. Why not take advantage of it? Sometimes we can struggle with doing busy mundane tasks. Many of us wear numerous hats and feel like we must do everything that everyone else needs without giving ourselves much thought. In return, we become depressed, overweight, lethargic, and desperate for a change. Today is the perfect day for that change. Today is the new beginning of a life you've wanted for a long time. Today is the perfect day to make the changes you want to make. Don't be afraid to take a risk and transform your life into what you want it to be. It's the only way that you can truly be happy and fulfilled.

What transformation do you want to make today?

May 22nd

"Every minute doing one thing is a minute not doing something else. Every choice is another choice not made."
– Jerry Weintraub, *When I Stop Talking, You'll Know I'm Dead: Useful Stories from a Persuasive Man*

We can't be angry and happy at the same time. We can't save money to pay off our debt and go on a shopping spree at the same time. We can't lose weight while we're enjoying a dozen donuts. One action or emotion takes the place of another and the results are quite different. In other words, we can't have our cake and eat it too. There are consequences and lost opportunities with every decision and action that we take. We must keep our objectives and our goals in mind when we make our daily choices. Are those choices and actions moving us towards what we want in life or away from it? Sometimes our choices put up a direct obstacle, getting in the way of us achieving success. We're self-sabotaging our goals. We need to concentrate and take the opportunities for success when they're given to us and stop getting in our own way. When we make one choice, we're deciding to not make another.

What good choices will you make today?

May 23rd

"Your feelings wouldn't get hurt if you were honest with yourself."
- Tye Lewis

It's just a little cupcake, no one will notice. It's just a little white lie, no one will notice. It's just a few dollars, it won't matter. We lie to ourselves every day. We endlessly justify our actions when we know they are wrong. We constantly make bad choices and then wonder why we're not getting the results we want. It takes an extreme amount of discipline to be successful in life. It takes hard work and perseverance to live the life you want to live. If it was easy, everyone would be rich, healthy, and happy. But we know that this is not the world we live in. There are problems that everyone must face. There are realities that must be met. The first step we must take is to be honest with ourselves. We must know the truth in where we're starting so we know where we want to go. We must admit we have a problem and then figure out the steps to get out of our unhappiness.

What do you need to be honest about?

May 24th

We can be bitter, or we can be better. Those words are my North Star."
– Caryn Sullivan, *Bitter Or Better: Grappling with Life on the Op-Ed Page*

Bad things happen to all of us. Our spouse or partner asks for a divorce and leaves us. Our son dents the car door. Megan gets the promotion over us. Things happen. We can bitch and complain about them or we can learn from them. We can wallow in our grief and sadness or we can brush ourselves off and decide to take a different course of action. Outside situations can only affect us if we let them. Failure should never define us. Our attitude should be one of increasing and never ending improvement. We are tested on a daily basis. We can either overcome our tests or we can let them hinder our progress. It's all up to us. We can be bitter and feel hopeless and play the victim, or we can become better and eventually invincible. It's a matter of attitude and mindset.

How will you face the day?

May 25th

"Notice the difference between being in control and needing control."
- Marilyn Suttle

Women tend to be bossy. We can be opinionated and gossip. We can stick our noses in situations that don't involve us. Why? Is it because we are curious? Is it because we want to impress others with our knowledge? Or is it because we lack control in our own lives? Or maybe because we're not confident and are looking for outside approval? No matter what, we must realize that we can only control what goes on within our own lives. We can influence others, but it's up to them to make the change or take the action. We can only control ourselves. Our thoughts, our feelings, our words, and our actions. When we realize this, it can free us from worrying about what goes on with other people. We now have more time, more energy, and less stress to live our own life the way we see fit. We don't have to impress anyone or try to control what they do. We can sit back and relax and watch as the world happens around us. Don't you feel relieved?

Are you in control of your life?

May 26th

"Before preparing to improve the world, first look around your home three times."-Chinese Proverb

It's easy for us to see our family's mess. It's easy to criticize someone else. It's easy to judge someone else's actions. But when was the last time you looked at your own life with the same judgment? The same criticism? If we're willing to give our opinions on someone else's life, we had better not have the same problems in our own life. What can we do to make things better in our own home? Do we need to declutter and get rid of some of our stuff? What can we do to be a better friend? What can we do to be a better spouse and lover? What can we do to be a better mom? What can we do to be a better worker? What do we need to learn to be in better shape? How can we get control of our finances and start to build wealth? Can we stop comparing ourselves to others and be content with what we have and who we are? It's a good thing to stop looking at the world around us and to look at the world that we created for ourselves. This way we can focus on things that can actually make a difference in our own lives and we can become the best women we can be.

What do you have to improve in your own life?

May 27th

"My mother is my root, my foundation. She planted the seed that I base my life on, and that is the belief that the ability to achieve starts in your mind."
-Michael Jordan

What if you could raise a child that becomes a legend? What if you could raise a child that could be a celebrity? What if you could raise a child that could be successful? Every child has the potential to be great and to live to their potential. But they need to believe that they can do it and that belief starts with what you're telling them at a young age. If you feed them nonsense and limiting thinking, they'll carry that with them into adulthood. But if you feed them encouragement and unlimited possibility thinking, then they will grow up thinking the sky's the limit. Nurturing their creativity and self-image is the most important thing a mother can do for her child. Even if their ideas are crazy and far-fetched, encourage them to go after their dreams. You never know what they can accomplish.

How can you help your child succeed today?

May 28th

"He who has a reason to live can bear almost any how."
-Friedrich Nietzsche

Most women fail to achieve their goals because their reasons for pursuing them aren't strong enough. If you really want to change something in your life, you need not only motivation pushing you to start moving, but you also need a reason for pulling you towards the goal. Motivation will fade over time. Willpower will diminish over time. But a strong vision and desire to accomplish the goal will never fade as long as you focus on the vision of the outcome every day. Yes, it will be difficult. Yes, it will take a lot of energy. Yes, it will be inconvenient. Yes, you will stumble. Yes, it will take time. Yes, it will take perseverance. Yes, you will hear the naysayers. But if you really want it, you'll find a way to get it. You'll get up early to work on it. You'll stay up late to work on it. You'll open your mind to new and different ideas and change your self-limiting beliefs. You'll learn how to be the person you want to be. You'll learn what it takes. You'll learn what you have to give up. You'll continue making progress every day until one day you'll wake up and tell yourself you did it. And that will be a great day!

What is your reason for living your best life?

May 29th

"My value as a woman is not measured by the size of my waist or the number of men who like me. My worth as a human being is measured on a higher scale: a scale of righteousness and piety. And my purpose in life-despite what fashion magazines say-is something more sublime than just looking good for men."

-Yasmin Mogahed, *Reclaim Your Heart*

The only way for women to live equally to men is to live our own lives. Men are encouraged to go out and conquer the world. Men are allowed to follow their ambitions and desires without ridicule and judgment. Men aren't' measured by their appearance, but rather by their accomplishments. Their success comes from their own efforts and not by the influences of others. Their strength comes from their confidence and not their physical ability. Their ambition drives them to do whatever it takes to achieve their goals. They are free to live the life they want to live without their families or society holding them back. No matter where they live, they are free to pursue their dreams and goals. In order for us to have the same privileges, we must start thinking and acting the same way. We must feel free to pursue our goals without limitations that our families and society often place on us. Then and only then can we live equal lives.

What is your purpose in life?

May 30th

"The circle of an empty day is brutal and at night it tightens around your neck like a noose."
-Elena Ferrante, *The Days of Abandonment*

Time is finite for us. As we age, time seems to speed up. We tend to spend our days doing activities that aren't important or even matter to us. Sometimes we look up at the clock and wonder where the day went. Did we do anything that mattered to us? Did we accomplish anything important? Did we do anything that would take us closer to our goals? In order to accomplish anything important, you must identify the results you want to achieve. Then start blocking out time every day to work on those goals. If you spend some time every day doing the things you want to do, working on your health, your wealth, and your relationships, you'll find that your time is no longer wasted and you'll rest at night with the feeling of accomplishment.

What do you want to accomplish today?

May 31st

"Above all, be the heroine of your life, not the victim."
-Nora Ephron

We all play different roles in our lives. Daughters, mothers, wives, best friends, and bosses. The one role that doesn't serve us is victim. If we blame others for the lives that we're leading, we allow the outside world to control us. No one should control us except ourselves. We need to take responsibility for our money. We need to take responsibility for our family's well being. We need to take responsibility for our relationships. We need to take responsibility for our health. The decisions or lack of decisions that we make or don't make is directly responsible for the results we are getting. If we don't like the results that we are getting, we need to start making better choices and embrace the fact that we can create the life that we want to live and no one else. We can make anything happen. The world is our oyster, but it takes smart choices and lots of energy in planning the correct path to take. But in the end, it all starts with us.

How will you play the heroine in your life today?

June

Hey Lady,

It's summertime! This is my favorite time of the year. I love getting home from work and having hours and hours of sunlight still left in my day. I love to focus on spending as much time with my family as possible. I love to plan fun things and spend my time sweating and exercising my body.

What about you? What fun plans do you have this summer? Are you going anywhere with your family? Are you planning any fun cookouts with friends? Don't let the beautiful weather wither away. It will soon be cold and dark again. Reach out to others and make plans that will create fun memories for all.

June 1st

"Be kind, for everyone you meet is fighting a hard battle."
-Socrates

You never know who is having a bad day. Someone somewhere is going through a crisis. Maybe it's your waitress that messed up your order. Maybe it's your coworker who is running late for the presentation that you were both supposed to present together. Maybe it's your spouse who keeps losing his temper everytime you speak. Step above it all and give grace. Be nice. It doesn't cost you anything to give the other person the benefit of the doubt. Maybe they're scared. Maybe they're worried. Maybe they are sick and just trying to get through their day. Grace. Compassion. As women, we are more likely to give others our compassion and grace.

Today's challenge is to give grace and compassion to someone who needs it. Can you do that?

June 2nd

"A kind word is a form of charity."
-Prophet Muhammad

Everyone loves a compliment. Encouragement. Support. How do you feel when someone says something nice to you? Warm inside? A wave of delight? Confident? We all want to be noticed. We all want to belong. We all want to feel unique and special. This all can start with a kind word. Noticing something about someone else that maybe they don't hear all the time. "You look nice." "I love those shoes." "You did a great job today." "Thank you for helping me." It's those simple things that add up. It's those simple things that can make a difference. It's those simple things that matter. When we give, we receive and it makes us feel great. That's a universal truth. It's Karma. So, why not start your day by making someone else's day with a kind word? A compliment? A *Thank you.*

What kind word or compliment will you give someone today?

June 3rd

"Women are not going to be equal outside the home until men are equal in it."
-Gloria Steinem

How many men do you know wash dishes? Clean the house? Do their own laundry? If they have girlfriends or partners, not many. We live in the 21st century, but for some reason, women bear the load of chores and housekeeping. We organize. We declutter. We scrub. We dust. We vacuum. We wash. The women's movement was to free women from the home so that they could realize their talents and skills. But many women struggle doing two jobs every day: having a career and keeping the house. We work all day and come home in order to clean and pick up our house for two hours every night. We rush home so we can cook dinner and help our children with their homework. We rush home so we can run our children to soccer practice. We rush home so we can bake cupcakes for the birthday party on Saturday. We feel obligated to do it all. We feel strained to take care of all the things that other people expect us to accomplish. But why do we have to face this burden alone? Don't we have partners that can help? Why can't our partners help us? Why can't they wash the dishes and mop the floors? Why can't they help us divide and conquer all the things that need to get done? They can but we need to ask for help. We need to allow them to help. We need to give up control and accept the help that's offered. We need to hand off the burden.

What chores need to be done today? What chores can my partner do to help me?

June 4th

"Your mind will take the shape of what you frequently hold in thought, for the human spirit is colored by such impressions."
–Marcus Aurelius, *Meditations 5.16.*

This is the Law of Attraction. You attract into your life what you think about all day. Your thoughts attract energy from the Universe and create the reality that you live in. If you're always thinking about lack and what you don't have, you will attract more lack and things you don't have. If you worry and are anxious about everything, you will attract more things into your life to worry about. On the other hand, if you're positive and only think positive thoughts, the Universe will take care of you and send good things and people your way. You will attract positive situations that can lead to love, wealth, and happiness.

What's one good thought you can think today that could attract something positive you want in your life?

June 5th

"Change the way you look at things and the things you look at change."
- Wayne W. Dyer

There are two sides to every coin as well as two sides to every situation. Which side are you looking at? If you're typically cynical or negative, you'll look through that perspective. If you're typically hopeful and positive, you'll look through that perspective. We live our lives through our perspective. We form opinions and take certain actions according to our beliefs. Those actions give us the results we see all around us. If we can take a step back and know that there's another side to the coin, we can look for ways to change the situation we face. There's always a way around an obstacle. There's always a solution to the problem. But sometimes we must take a step back and look for a different answer. A different way of handling a situation. A different idea or opinion. Constantly looking for different ideas and solutions can open a world of possibility and can quickly solve life's most challenging problems.

Is there a current problem that needs a new perspective?

June 6th

"Live like no one else, so you can live and give like no one else."
–Dave Ramsey

78% of Americans live paycheck to paycheck. But it doesn't have to be this way. Paying off any consumer debt- credit cards, student loans, car loans, and finally mortgages help to free you from the shackles that debt has on you. If you don't have any obligatory payments to other companies, then you can do what you want with your money. You can save it. You can invest it. You can give to charity. You can spend it. If you've always wanted to be debt-free, today is the day to get started. Go to Ramseysolutions.com and sign up for the Financial Peace University and learn how to use money to live the life you want.

What's the first debt you're going to make an extra payment on today?

June 7th

"If a man who can't count finds a four leaf clover, is he lucky?"
-Stanisław Lem

Luck is nothing more than putting yourself in the way of opportunity. If you are a team member and go above and beyond what you need to do for the project and your company day after day, don't you think your boss will notice? If you watch what you eat and work out consistently, won't you feel full of energy and vitality? If you invest your money year after year, won't you start to see compound interest do its magic? Are these scenarios luck, or are they practical means to an end? Wishing something to happen is worthless. Taking practical action towards your dreams can manifest them any day of the week.

What steps can you put into motion today to manifest your dream life?

June 8th

"The rarest of all human qualities is consistency."
- Jeremy Bentham

Remember the story of the Tortoise and the Hare? In the end, the tortoise wins. Success in any area of our lives can happen assuredly if we act like the tortoise. Every day we take action. Every day we work hard. Every day we improve our skills. Every day we strive for more. When we're consistent in our thoughts, we can be consistent in our actions. Consistency brings certainty. Our goals will be achieved if we keep going after them. We don't stop. We don't quit. We keep clawing our way to the top. At some point, we'll find it. At some point, we'll succeed. But we can't get off track. We can't allow others to distract us from our mission. We can't allow obstacles and setbacks to halt our progress. Success comes to those who consistently take the actions necessary to fulfill their desires. Who works at it. Who doesn't take 'no' for an answer.

Write your 'To Do' list for today. Do these actions align with your goals?

June 9th

"Life is not about living the safer option. Life is about living a life worth living."
– Robert Thier, *Storm and Silence*

Women love certainty. We love to be safe. We want to be taken care of. But this makes us desperate, vulnerable, and dependent. Our lives are meant to have variety. To have challenges. To have excitement. It's not to take the safe route. It's not dull and mundane every day. Adventure awaits everyone. Is there something you've always wanted to do, but life got in your way? Maybe you wanted to travel somewhere. Maybe you wanted to go into a different career. Maybe you wanted to pick up a new hobby. Maybe you wanted to meet someone. Whatever adventure you want to take, now is the time to take it. Don't wait until something else happens to start bringing excitement in your life. The only time you're guaranteed is now.

What adventure can you plan today?

June 10th

"Whatever relationships you have attracted in your life at this moment, are precisely the ones you need in your life at this moment. There is a hidden meaning behind all events, and this hidden meaning is serving your own evolution."
-Deepak Chopra

Everyone you meet today could potentially help you. When you finish a project, another one can suddenly appear. When you open your eyes in the morning, you are blessed with a new day and a new start. Things can happen for a reason. That's called Karma or The Law of Cause and Effect. One thing causes another thing to happen. Meeting one person can help shape your life in a certain way. In order for us to grow and contribute, we need something from The Universe. That could be a new skill set our new mentor teaches us. That could be a health scare that puts us on the right path. That could be a networking event that could offer us a new job or contact. No matter what it is, there are opportunities to grow and contribute in every corner of the world. It is up to us to seek what's out there and to seize the opportunities as they come.

Who and what is in your life right now that has meaning?

June 11th

"It is one of the blessings of old friends that you can afford to be stupid with them."

-Ralph Waldo Emerson, *Emerson in His Journals*

When was the last time you got together with your old girlfriends? What did you do? Did you reminisce about something in the past? Did you giggle uncontrollably? Did you go dancing? Did you drink some wine? Did you go to a concert? Did you have a great time and thought to yourself, *we don't do this enough*? Old girlfriends are people you can let your hair down with and just be yourself. There's no competition. There's no fakeness. You can say and do what you want and you know for a fact, that they have your back. That doesn't mean they won't give their opinions on your actions, but they will love you unconditionally anyways. That's what old girlfriends are for. To remind you that life is good and there's always people that love you and support you.

When was your last GNO (Girls' Night Out)? Text your girls right now and set something up for this weekend.

June 12th

"A day without laughter is a day wasted."
- Nicolas Chamfort

Every day should be fun. You should enjoy what you do for work. Your family should bring you joy. You should feel loved in your relationships and friendships. You should laugh. You should act silly once in a while. You should crack a joke. You should do a little dance. Not because you want to make someone laugh, but because you want to have fun and feel alive. Having fun every day makes the hard times not so hard. Laughing releases endorphins that give us that spark we need to keep going.

Did you laugh today?

June 13th

"How wonderful it is that nobody needs to wait a single moment before starting to improve the world."

–Anne Frank, *Anne Frank's Tales from the Secret Annex: A Collection of Her Short Stories, Fables, and Lesser-Known Writings*

We can change our minds instantly. We can take action instantly. We can start to change something we hate in our lives instantly. If we make a decision to help someone, we can do it now. If we make a decision to live the life we deserve and stop settling for mediocrity, we can do it now. We won't get the results we want instantly, but we can take the first step towards change right now.

What can you do today to improve the world?

June 14th

"Who we are now is all that really matters."
- Amy Joy, *The Academie*

What we are today is an accumulation of all the thoughts and actions we've taken in the past. All of the good and bad decisions we've made. All the choices we faced. All the lessons we've learned. All the obstacles we overcame. Today you are the person you're meant to be at this point. But that doesn't mean that you need to stay the same person. If you want to become a different person and lead a different life, you can change the results you get by taking different actions. By networking with different people. By taking a different path. Become aware of what is right and what is wrong with your life today and figure out what you want to change and what you want to remain the same.

What is good in your life? What is bad in your life?

June 15th

"Life makes you pay. Everybody pays something."
-Min Jin Lee, *Pachinko*

Everything costs us. We spend our time, our energy, our money, and our opportunities. If we spend our resources on one thing, sometimes we don't have enough to spend it on something else. If we're spending our time doing work, we can't spend time with our kids. If we're spending our money on material unneeded things, we can't save it to invest in our future. If we spend our evening watching TV, we can't declutter and organize our kitchen. Life makes us pay with every decision and choice we make.

What price are you going to pay today?

June 16th

"Fate isn't one straight road. There are forks in it, many different routes to different ends. We have the free will to choose the path."
–Dean Koontz, *Odd Thomas*

We all have to make decisions. No one can get away without making a choice that has results and consequences. Success is never a straight line. Neither is destitution. Neither is building wealth. Neither is having a happy, loving 30 year marriage. One decision leads to another step in a certain direction. At any time, we can take a different path or continue on with the path that lays before us. It's all up to us to decide which way we want to go.

What decision that you've been holding off on can you make today?

June 17th

"The most powerful magic of all is choice."
– Sara Raasch, *Ice Like Fire*

We are so lucky to live in a time and place as we do. As women, we have been oppressed, tortured, and controlled for centuries. We're still not at the level we should be, but we do have freedoms that our foremothers only dreamt of. The biggest freedom we have is choice. We can choose to live our lives as we see fit. We can work towards our dreams. We can be healthy and have a loving relationship. We can choose to have a family or not and prioritize what activities we participate in or not. Our thoughts are our own. Our feelings can be openly expressed. If we don't like how something is going, we have the freedom to choose something different. It's a wonderful thing to be able to decide for ourselves how we're going to spend our time on this planet. We should all take the fullest advantage of this privilege.

What choices are you going to make today?

June 18th

"One resolution I have made, and always try to keep, is this: 'To rise above little things'."
— John Burroughs

Sometimes the little things weigh us down because they can build upon themselves. We have fifteen things to do on our list. Multiple people remark negatively on your outfit. Traffic is terrible going to work and back home. There's a never ending burrage of negativity coming your way. What do we do when our day is not going as planned? We focus on our reason for doing all of this. Why are we putting up with all of this? It's because we want to take care of our families. It's because we want to get that promotion and more money. It's because we want to express our creativity and our uniqueness. We will always have obstacles trying to knock us off our focus, we must get around them and keep moving forward. We must keep our eye on the goal and not allow anything, even the small things to deter us from improving our lives and living the way we see fit.

What little things will you ignore today?

June 19th

"I hear you say 'Why?' Always 'Why?' You see things; and you say 'Why?' But I dream of things that never were; and I say 'Why not?"
-George Bernard Shaw, *Back to Methuselah*

We often question the validity of something. Sometimes we come to the conclusion that something can't be done. We can't do it. It's not meant to be for us. We've made up our minds to the impossibility of it. When this happens, we've closed ourselves off from actually accomplishing it. We've told the Universe that we don't want it, so don't bother helping me get it. When we ask ourselves, "Why not?" We open the floodgates of possibilities. When we ask ourselves, "How can I?" We open our minds to finding ways of solving the problem. Our subconscious minds are always trying to validate our reality. If we think something is possible for us, our subconscious mind constantly looks for ways of making it possible. It searches for all of the answers to the problems, it opens up our creative faculties, and continues to find ways for us to live our best lives. Never, ever tell yourself that something is impossible. Always, always ask yourself how you can find a way and the way will be shown to you.

How can you solve your biggest problem today?

June 20th

"A really strong woman accepts the war she went through and is ennobled by her scars."
-Carly Simon

We all go through battles. We fight with our spouses. We fight with our children. We fight with ideas and colleagues at work. We fight for what we think is right. We are constantly getting around obstacles and roadblocks that are in our way. At some point we get burnt out from all the fighting. This is when the calm comes over us. This is when our minds rest. This is the time we can relax and look back at all the hard fought battles that we've gone through. And then we realize it's only Wednesday and we need to get back in the battle for the rest of the week. It's okay, we all do it. We're busy women. Take some time today and reflect on all the wonderful things you've accomplished. You did it! You've won! If you didn't win the war, at least you won a battle here and there. Give yourself a break, get some rest, and get ready to get back in there tomorrow! You're a winner!

What battles are you going through right now?

June 21st

"Do you know where your breakthrough begins? Your breakthrough begins where your excuses end."
-Patience Johnson, *Why Does an Orderly God Allow Disorder*

We create excuses out of fear. We create excuses out of spite. We create excuses because we don't think we can solve the problem. We create excuses because we're lazy. We create excuses because we know that others will accept them. Why do we constantly sell ourselves short like that? If we'd stop using our creativity to make excuses and use it to create possibilities, we'd all be successful women. We'd all be in shape. We'd all be wealthy. There's not an excuse on Earth that's legitimate yet we look for them every day. We are good enough. We are worthy. We deserve nothing but the best. But all of those things take strength and perseverance to obtain. They all take hard work. They all take creativity to go up against the obstacles and problems that get in our way. But we can do it! There's no problem that's too big to solve! There's no obstacle that's too difficult to get around. There's no goal that's too big to accomplish. Yes, it may take some time to accomplish. Yes it may take a lot of money and energy to solve. But what is your life about? Is it about the talent of making excuses or is it about living a meaningful and fulfilled life full of accomplishments? That's for you to decide.

What excuses are you making?

June 22nd

"But kids don't stay with you if you do it right. It's the one job where, the better you are, the more surely you won't be needed in the long run."

– Barbara Kingsolver, *Pigs in Heaven*

If you're lucky enough to be a mother, you instinctively know your job. Your main purpose is to raise a self-sufficient adult. This almighty job includes sharing your love, kindness, and strength with them. It entails empowering them with their own creativity and drive. We show them how to be disciplined and strong. We teach them manners and morals. We show them our culture and religious ideas that they can carry onto the next generation. We support them and encourage them. We show them by example what a meaningful life looks like. And once we've done all of that, we let them go to explore the world on their terms knowing that we've given them all the skills we possess. Motherhood is such a wonderful and precious thing. Enjoy every moment you have with your children!

What plans do you have with your children this week?

June 23rd

"No age of life is inglorious. Youth has its merits, but living to a ripe old age is the true statement of value. Aging is the road that we take to discern our character. Fame and fortune can elude us, but character is immortal. We must encounter a sufficient variety of experiences including both failures and accomplishments in order to gain nobility of character."
– Kilroy J. Oldster, *Dead Toad Scrolls*

Every decade of our life has its challenges. When we're in our 20s, we're on our own for the first time and truly need to figure out how the world works and our place in it. In our 30s, we find a strong foothold in the world and we begin to have long term relationships, careers, and families. Our focus starts to wane from ourselves to our families. In our 40s, our children are getting older and finding their own personalities and we again start to focus on ourselves and what we want to accomplish in our life. Our 50s are focused on giving back and figuring out what all of it means to us. Take some time to reflect on your life and all of the wonderful things you've accomplished. Remember the people that have stood by you along the way. Feel the love and support that surrounds you. Close your eyes and continue to dream of what you want your life to be. We may all get wrinkled and worn, but our spirit can never wither!

What accomplishments have you earned?

June 24th

"Getting old isn't for sissies."
-Main Character of *And Then There's Margaret*

Being a woman isn't for sissies either. Women are the strongest creatures on Earth. We clean up the messes. We nurture the broken. We dream of peace. We win over the doubtful. We connect the world. We do all of these things while going through the aging process. We battle the bulge. We smooth the wrinkles. We color the gray. We eat salads and drink wine. We do all of these things while laughing and enjoying the ride with our girlfriends. We do all of these things while crying and grieving with our families. We face life's challenges with grace and the dignity of strong women. We believe in the hope of tomorrow and the will of our children. We know that being a woman isn't easy, but we take it on with the pride and fierceness of a caged tiger. We must learn never to back down from a fight and to persevere no matter what obstacles are laid before us. As we get older, we get wiser from the experiences we've had. We must use that wisdom to achieve bigger and better things.

What lessons have you learned thus far?

June 25th

"It's easy to say you don't care about money when you have plenty of it."
–Ransom Riggs, *Miss Peregrine's Home for Peculiar Children*

Everyone should care about money. We should appreciate it. We should take care of it. We should multiply it. We should tell it where to go. If money isn't important in your life it's either because you have plenty of it, or you're so miserable, you don't think you'll ever have any of it. I'd rather act like the former. Saving your money and growing it is a talent that every woman needs to learn. We shouldn't have to work like dogs for the rest of our lives and have nothing to show for it. If we live within our means and invest in assets that pay us a return, then we won't be worried about money on a daily basis because it's working for us instead of us working for it.

How can you take better care of your money?

June 26th

"When you talk you are only repeating what you already know, But if you listen, you may learn something new.
-Dalai Lama

Women tend to give their opinions about everything, even if no one asks. It's not our fault, that's the way we're wired. But if we shut up for a moment and listen to people that actually know what's going on, and not give their uneducated opinions, we can learn the facts of the situation that can allow us to correctly interpret the situation. It's in the facts and not the hearsay that we can grow and improve. It's in the facts that can help us lead successful fulfilling lives. It's in the facts that can lead us down the right path. Don't we all want to live with less friction and less controversy? An easy way to do this is to become educated and stop gossiping about things that we truly don't know about.

What do you need to learn today from an expert?

June 27th

"The person who is his own master cannot tolerate another boss."
-Chinese Proverb

Sometimes we allow others to influence our lives. We listen to the thousands of marketing messages that tell us we're not good enough unless we buy their products. We compare ourselves to those around us and try to keep up with them. We believe that we're supposed to be a certain way and do certain things because our families have expectations for us. But does this sound like a life you really want to live? Of course not! It's time to stand up for yourself and start to live your own life. If that means you must ignore your family, do it. If that means that you must move to another part of the world and start a career you've always wanted to pursue, then do it. If that means you need to start hanging out with different people that can help you learn and grow, then do it. Control what you can control and let the rest go as it may. When you're in control of your own life, you'll feel less stressed and more willing to learn and explore the vast world we live in. Now is the time to escape and live the life you're meant to live. Don't walk in someone's shadow. Create your own sunshine.

How can you control your life today?

June 28th

"I'm not unhappy," he said. "Only people with no purpose are unhappy. I've got a purpose."
– Cassandra Clare, *City of Bones*

What's your purpose? That's a big question to tackle in the morning but it's an important question to answer. If we don't have a purpose, we spend our lives aimlessly. We don't have a clear direction. We don't know what we're supposed to do. Without purpose we really don't know what makes us happy and how we're supposed to respond to a situation. Fulfillment and meaning walk hand in hand with purpose. If we're driven to do something or be a certain way, we know what we're supposed to do today. We know how to think, we know how to act, and we know what results we should expect. If we don't have a purpose, we don't really know what to do and we find ourselves depressed and lost. How do we know if we have a hidden talent if we aren't forced to use it? How do we know how strong we are if we're not forced to show it? How do we know how wealthy we can become if we're not forced to build it? Finding our purpose, the reason we're living forces us to expose our talents and will power to the world. Finding our purpose forces us out of bed and into the adventure that seeks us. If we want to be happy in life, we've got to look for the reasons that make us happy and dedicate our lives to pursuing those reasons on a daily basis.

What's your purpose?

June 29th

" Memento mori. (Remember you will die.) You could leave life right now, let that determine what you do and say and think."
- Marcus Aurelius, *Meditations-2.11*

It's good to be reminded of death. We all face it. We all have a finite time on this planet. We shouldn't dwell on the impending silence that awaits all of us, but we should embrace the gift of time that we've been given. We're alive! We're free to explore our wants and needs. We can laugh. We can love. We can cry if we want to. We can eat great food. We can play with our children. We can dream. We can explore our hobbies. We can try and fail. We can love. We can win. We can lose. We can learn new things. We can play our favorite songs. We can dance. We can have sex. We can snuggle. We can feel the warmth of the sun on our skin. We can feel the cool Fall breeze through our hair. We can smell our grandma's famous cookies. We can watch our children grow. We get to do so many things! Today, realize that you're alive and you get to make the most of it. Be grateful for the time you have and don't waste it on things that don't matter to you.

How can you live your fullest today?

June 30th

"Change your habits, change your life."
–Stephanie Aldrich, *The Habit Formula*

Our daily routines become habitual. We tend to do the same things everyday and get the same results. We drive to work the same way. We cook the same way. We do laundry the same way. We clean the house the same way. We eat the same way. But what if we want to improve or change something in our life? The change will never happen if we're taking the same results. Those results were caused by the actions we're taking now. But if we take different actions, we can end up with different results. Focus on the changes you want to make and learn the steps you must take to find the changes you desire.

What habit must I break to make the change I desire?

July

Hey Lady,

How's the summer going so far? Are you having fun with your friends and families? Have you built any memories yet? What about your goals? Have you been working on them? You should be part way there already if you've been focusing on improvement. That's awesome! Keep it going! You're heading towards the finish line.

If you haven't been working on your goals, now is a great time to pick it back up. You still have plenty of time to make progress before the end of the year. Go outside, sit on the deck, and create a plan for the rest of the year. Create a vision of what you're doing and what the end of the year looks like. Close your eyes and listen to the birds chirping and smell the fresh-cut grass and realize that you're alive and you should be taking full advantage of it. Live the life you want and don't allow obstacles to get in your way.

July 1st

"When we give someone our time, we actually give a portion of our life that we will never take back." - Alexander the Great

Believe it or not but your time is your most precious resource. Not money. Not energy. Not anything else. Time. Do you really know how much time you have left? Or even how much your time is worth? When you help someone, it's usually traded with your time and knowledge. When you're playing with your kids, you're creating memories with that time. When you're holding hands with your spouse, you're deepening your relationship with them. Time is the most important thing you can spend. But for many women, we waste it. We concentrate on idle gossip. We spend hours and hours shopping for things we don't really need or can afford to buy. We constantly compare ourselves with others that have more. It's an endless time-wasting game and it must stop today! We must realize that the moments we spend are gone forever. We can never get them back. We can always get more money. We can always buy more stuff. We can always make new friends. But we can never create more time. We all have the same 24 hours in a day. It's what we do with those 24 hours that matters. What we do with our time determines whether we have a fulfilled life or not. We must guard our time and only give it to the people in our lives that deserve it.

How can you get back your time? What do you need to stop doing?

July 2nd

"Care about what other people think and you will always be their prisoner."
– Lao Tzu

Keeping up with the Joneses is a real thing to some. Women often compare themselves to other women. *She's more beautiful. She's got bigger boobs. She's married to a rich man. She drives a Beemer.* Whatever you're saying to yourself needs to stop. You are perfect the way you are. There are people out there that treasure you. Your style. Your looks. Your talents and skills. The way you walk. The way you talk. You have so much to give to this world. You are truly unique. Wow! Doesn't that feel good? Don't you feel better that you don't have to compete with anyone anymore? It should feel exhilarating! You should feel relief! You should feel energized to finally say enough is enough and I'm going to do things my way. And you should. You're special, and you're worthy!

Who will you stop comparing yourself to?

July 3rd

"Women are the largest untapped reservoir of talent in the world."
-Hillary Clinton

There are so many places in the world that still do not value women. Our thoughts. Our ideas. Our talents. Our strengths. Most western countries have fought for the rights of women but there's still so much we can do. We must fight against injustice. We must fight to make our planet a better place to live. We must fight against inequality. We must fight against rape. We must fight for our say on the issues that matter to us. We must fight for our children, our free will, and our free speech. We must stop allowing marketing and large corporations to influence us and make us feel bad about ourselves in order to buy their products. We must influence industry with our creativity. We must fight for a better tomorrow.

What can you do today to make your voice heard?

July 4th

"We should take wandering outdoor walks, so that the Mind might be nourished and refreshed by the open-air and deep breathing."
-Seneca

Take a walk. Go outside and walk the dog. Put on some headphones and listen to your favorite music. Smell the fresh air. Get some exercise. Let your mind wonder. We all need a break every day from our hectic routines. We constantly go, go, go. In order to be our best selves, we must take a step back and free our minds of our problems, worries, and anxieties. It's in these quiet moments that we can reconnect with our true selves. In these quiet moments we can connect with God and The Universe. An idea may pop into our mind that could solve a problem we've been dealing with for the past month. A feeling of calmness and serenity could swelter our anxiousness. There's a lot that can happen during a daily walk. We could reconnect with an old friend. We could reconnect with our child. We could reconnect with our lover all by taking a nice, leisurely walk with them. Take some time and be one with nature.

When will I take my walk this week?

Monday

Tuesday

Wednesday

Thursday

Friday

Saturday

Sunday

July 5th

"The inner fire is the most important thing mankind possesses."
-Edith Södergran

Without our inner fire, we would still be locked up in our homes. Because some brave women wanted more out of life than being just housewives, we have the luxury of finding our true selves and sharing our talents with the world. It takes courage and ambition to move the needle of society. We are still oppressed and are not viewed as equal by men. They think that because they have physical strength that they can run all over us. That we don't matter. That we don't deserve to be wealthy, healthy, and happy. But it's the 21st century, and we should take the time to show everyone that we have the fire and ambition to have, be, and do anything we want. To climb any mountain. To accomplish any goal. But all of those results that we want to accomplish start with our thoughts and beliefs that we can achieve those results. We need to have courage and excitement in order to accomplish our dreams. And it all starts inside.

What are you passionate about? What are you doing to manifest that passion?

July 6th

"Precious treasure and oil are in a wise man's dwelling, but a foolish man devours it."
-Proverbs 21:20

Smart women are planners. They are savers. They always have a rainy day fund. They save in their retirement plans. They form a budget and tell their money where to go instead of wondering where it went. They are wise with their money. They know the value of the hard work they put in aways from their families. They know the value of their time. That's wisdom. Not everyone has that wisdom, but sooner or later, all women will learn the lessons of money. Some learn it the hard way through debt, bankruptcy, or poverty. Others learn to build wealth by using ancient wisdom that others have spread generation after generation. What side of the coin are you on?

What can you do today to start building your wealth?

July 7th

"The only thing standing between you and your dreams is reluctance."
-Carroll Bryant

Fear. Hesitation. Doubt. These are the things holding you back. It's not the outside world that presents unobtainable results, it's you. It's your mindset. It's your lack of confidence. It's your lack of ambition. It's your lack of knowledge in how to get around the obstacle before you. You can have anything you want. We live in one of the best nation's on Earth. We have freedoms that most women never had. We can be, do, or have anything we want. But we hesitate. Why? Because we lack support. Because we have people around us that doubt us. It only takes one person believing in you to open the confidence floodgates. It only takes one person who is there to listen and who can help you when times get tough. If you believe in yourself, then you can do anything no matter how crazy or far-fetched it sounds. Take the first step and see where it takes you.

Who do you need in your life that can support you and help you?

July 8th

"To exist is to change, to change is to mature, to mature is to go on creating oneself endlessly."
- Henri Bergson

We are meant to change. We are meant to grow and improve. That's who we are. That's how Mother Nature intended. We mature by knowledge and experience. Everyone has different paths they choose to take but everyone has a choice. We can always change our minds and take another path. As we open our minds to new ideas and beliefs, we can change the actions we take to get different results. It all starts with us getting out of our safety nets and exploring what the world has to offer us. The daily decisions we make affect the lives we lead over time. It's okay to be unhappy with the outcomes of your choices. We all have the power to change things when we realize that our lives aren't stagnant, they are evolving into new and better ways. Take some time today and reflect on some changes you want to make.

What are some changes you want to make in your life?

July 9th

"Happiness consists in frequent repetition of pleasure"
-Arthur Schopenhauer

Happiness is a state of mind. It's a feeling of satisfaction. A feeling of contentment. But it's only a feeling. An emotion that can dissipate over time. That's why it's very important to consistently rejuvenate that emotion. To do things that you love. To be around the people you love. To surround yourself with things that you love. Then you can experience happiness every day. If you're stuck in a dead end job, does that make you happy? If you're in a bad relationship, does that make you happy? Do you try to escape so you can feel some relief? If so, that means there's no happiness in your environment. You've got to change it. Think about the things and people that you love and start surrounding yourself with those things. Then and only then will you be happy.

What brings you joy and happiness? Who do you love? What do you love to do?

July 10th

"Finish each day and be done with it. You have done what you could. Some blunders and absurdities no doubt crept in; forget them as soon as you can. Tomorrow is a new day. You shall begin it serenely and with too high a spirit to be encumbered with your old nonsense."
- Ralph Waldo Emerson

Every day is a new day. Never live in the past. Yesterday you may have had a bad day. Don't repeat the past. Start today fresh and with a positive hopeful attitude. Learn from the mistakes you've made and don't repeat them. Make your 'To Do' list and cross off things one by one. This is a huge accomplishment and gets you closer to accomplishing your goals. But if you stumble and don't get everything done on your list, don't worry, tomorrow is a new day and you can start where you left off. Do the most you can do today and keep moving forward no matter what happens. Keep striving for your goals. Enjoy the process and be thankful you've come this far in the journey.

Name 3 things To Do today (professionally)

Name 3 things To Do today (personally)

July 11th

"The free mind, unafraid of labor, presses on to attain the good."
–Laura Cereta, *Collected Letters of a Renaissance Feminist*

If we want something, we must work for it. That's how The Universe works. We have to imagine what we want our life to look like and then we must put our heads down and do the work. Nothing will be given to you. You deserve nothing. You are entitled to nothing. If you want it, follow your desire and take the action necessary to obtain it. It's as though you must become a different person than your present self. Does the successful person do things differently than what you're doing now? Yes. Does the successful person surround themselves with different people than the people you're surrounding yourself with today? Yes. Does the successful person think differently than how you're thinking today? Yes. Become a successful person and you'll be living the life you deserve and have worked for. It won't be easy. It won't be fast. But if you take each step forward towards your goals, you will find them. One step at a time.

What does a successful person do differently than what you're doing?

July 12th

"Great losses are great lessons."
-Amit Kalantri, *Wealth of Words*

No one wins every time. No one succeeds on the first attempt. No one is great in the beginning. Isn't that freeing? Our lives are filled with lessons. Some lessons are easy to learn. Some lessons are difficult to get past. Some lessons are repeated and some are ingrained in our DNA to never, ever happen again. It's in these lessons that allow us to grow and improve. We get better in every way. Our intuition is heightened. Our experience expands. Our lives become enriched with knowledge that would otherwise go untapped. It's in the lessons that make us great. It's in the lessons that give us clarity on our path. It's in the lessons that give us strength.

What lessons can you learn from today?

July 13th

"Wisdom is being able to see the world for what it is, rather than what you want it to be."

-Patrick F. Rooney, *The Angel of Innisfree*

Sometimes our emotions get the best of us. We're women. We feel things. Sometimes they can overwhelm us. Sometimes they make us crazy. Sometimes they can make us do stupid things. Sometimes they make us say things we regret. Sometimes they bring out the worst in us. It's okay. We're all human. But at some point, our rational, logical self needs to start controlling the situation. The less emotional we can get about a situation, the better off we will be. It's okay to feel emotions, but we need to respond more logically and keep our emotions under control until we find the resolution. That tip alone can make our lives a little easier and smoother.

What situation can you look at differently today?

July 14th

"You cannot be remade unless you are first broken."
-Steven Erikson, *Deadhouse Gates*

In order to accomplish our goals, we must first become a different person. This new person will think and act differently. They will do things that your present self doesn't do or doesn't know how to do. This new person will go above and beyond to get the results she wants. This new person won't allow obstacles to hinder her progress. She won't allow negativity to get in her way. She will align herself with people that can help her get what she wants. She will live intentionally. She will be grateful for all that she's accomplished. She will love all the people that support her. She will feel fulfilled and proud. She will be great. But in order to become that woman, you must get rid of your present self. Maybe not all of her, but the parts that are stopping her from being the successful woman you desire to be. Only then, can progress and growth occur. Only then can you start living the life you truly desire. It's time to step up and get out of your better self's way and allow her to dominate.

What can you do today to take the first step towards your goals?

July 15th

"If I know who you spend your time with, then I know what might become of you."
- Johann Wolfgang von Goethe

Jim Rohn famously said the same thing. We are like the 5 people we spend the most time with. Look at your inner circle. What are these women like? Are they negative? Are they successful? Do they have loving families? Do they work? Are they liberals or conservatives? Are they healthy? What are their opinions of the world and other people? The network you surround yourself with helps to influence many aspects of your life. Some good and some bad. Are there other people you can start associating with that can help you improve and grow? Sometimes our inner circle needs to change. Sometimes our old friends don't represent the changes we want to make in our own lives. Sometimes we need to get rid of the distractions and obstacles that get in our way. This may include our inner circle. Sometimes we need to let them go and move onto bigger and better things. That doesn't mean we don't love them for who they are, but it means we can't be held to their same standards. Sometimes it's time to upgrade.

Who in your life must you let go of?

July 16th

"Never discourage anyone who continually makes progress, no matter how slow."
-Plato

Life is all about progress, not necessarily about the destination. It's who we become. It's how we change. It's about how we affect our families, our communities, and our countries. Sometimes our goals we set are out of reach. Sometimes they can take a lot of time, money, and energy to accomplish them. Sometimes our goals can be accomplished fast and easily. Either way, we must stay the course and never quit, no matter how many obstacles get in our way. We grow and get better each and every step we take towards our targets. That's what life is all about. Progress, not perfection. Perfection only creates doubt and worry. Progress creates confidence and adaptation. Learning the lessons that life has to teach us is important to be aware of. Open your eyes and see what life is teaching you right now and learn the lessons from the past so your mistakes aren't repeated.

What progress have you made towards your goals?

July 17th

"Too many people spend money they earned, to buy things they don't want, to impress people that they don't like."
-Will Rogers

We live in the most marketed country on the planet. It's estimated that we are bombarded with over 10,000 ads per day per person. That's a lot of persuasion. Their messages rely on our sense of confidence, or lack of. If we buy this, we could look better. If we buy that, we can feel better. If we do this, we can show it off to our neighbors and families. As women, we need to realize that a ½ off sale still means we need to fork over the other ½ for that item. We're still in the hole, so to speak. We're still spending our hard earned cash on something that may or may not be needed. Why spend that money? Why not save it and invest it in your future? Why not save it and pay off your debt? It's so freeing when you own everything you have and you owe no one anything. Let's get rid of the consumerist attitude and start feeling that we're great just the way we are without buying anything they want us to.

Can you not buy anything this week (besides groceries and gas)?

Yes **No**

July 18th

"Women can learn a lot through sharing. By sharing their good and bad experiences, women can inspire and support each other to help sharpen their skill."
-AR Parul Zaveri

It's a shame that in the twenty-first century that women are not more powerful. Why aren't we more prominent in our communities? Why aren't we more prominent in large industries? Why aren't we sharing our ideas and talents with the world? Are we not worthy? Are we not creative and talented? The answer may shock you. It's our fault. It's our fault that we are not more powerful. We have let men in the world dominate every aspect of life. We give them control of our households even though we contribute immensely and should have an equal say. We give them control of major industries and take a back seat to their visions of what they want the main company's roles to be. It's our own fault. We must use our strength and our knowledge and start living courageously. Just like men. We should be ambitious and solve the big problems in the world. We are just as good as they are in every aspect. We shouldn't allow anyone to control us or the narrative that enters our minds. We can do it, and we must raise strong women who can lead the way into the next decade and beyond.

How can we show our strength in this world?

July 19th

"Real change, enduring change, happens one step at a time."
-Ruth Bader Ginsburg

We all have our daily to-do list. Sometimes the list has three things on it and sometimes it has ten. We need to learn to give ourselves some grace and a break. Do we really need to get all ten things done today? Are they life and death matters? Or can we do the top two important things and finish the rest when we have the time and energy? Nine times out of ten, it's the latter. Yes, there are urgent things that must be taken care of right away. But most things on our list are mundane, busy tasks that may or may not move the needle of our success. Yes, the house needs to get cleaned. Yes, the laundry must be done. Yes, our project must get finished. Yes, the kids need to go to practice. But most of these things don't have to be done by us alone. Most of the things on our lists can be a group or family activity that we can all share the responsibility in. That's why we have friends to help us. That's why we have spouses, to help us. That's why we have kids to help us. That's why we have a team at work to help us. We don't have to be martyrs and super women. We can control the activities and delegate. That's how we can change things one step at a time. Nothing needs to get finished right now. Progress takes time.

What activities can we delegate today?

July 20th

"You don't develop courage by being happy in your relationships every day. You develop it by surviving difficult times and challenging adversity."
-Epicurus

Easy times are easy for everyone. It's wonderful when everything goes our way and it's easy to win. But what happens when things turn and it's not as easy to win. Do you have friends and family to help you? Do you have people that you can lean on and feel the support? Is your spouse there no matter what? People in general become stronger when some friction comes their way. They build strength through the trials and tribulations of experience. Just like a muscle, it must be stressed and torn in order to heal and become bigger and stronger. Our relationships are the same way. If we can face adversity and struggles together, our bonds of love and friendship heal and become better and stronger. It's through the bad times that teams are built. It's through the bad times that communities bond and become strong forces. It's through the bad times that the cream rises to the top. Never shy away from adversity. Take the struggle and use it to build wisdom and perseverance that no one can take away. Create discipline and mental strength that no one can break. Unite and defeat any adversity that comes your way.

Who is in your corner?

July 21st

"Time and Tide wait for no man."
- Geoffrey Chaucer

How we do one thing is how we do everything. If we waste time being busy but not productive, are we really busy? Doing productive things means that we're doing the activities that get us one step closer to our dreams and goals. Being productive brings in more money. Being productive saves us time. Being productive gives us more energy to do the things that matter to us. Being productive expands our network. It's the way we spend our time that makes us successful or average. The energy of the tide goes in and out without any of our help. We can either learn how to go with the flow, changing when we need to, and aligning our ideas with what the world needs us to do, or not. When we fight the current, we lose. When we develop our ideas and explore the relationships that can help us succeed, that's going with the tide. We are only here for a certain amount of time, how you use that time and energy is what will determine what you'll have in the end.

How are you spending your time today? Are you in alignment with your goals?

July 22nd

"A friend to all is a friend to none." -Aristotle

Women can tend to be catty with each other. Fake. Two faced. They may say something nice to someone's face and then condemn them behind their back to someone else. Why? You don't have to be friends with everyone at all times. Most people aren't worthy of your friendship if you truly are a good friend. If you're reliable, trustworthy, fair, and giving, then you're a good friend. Surround yourself with other women that can stand behind you no matter what trials and tribulations you find yourself in. If they help you through your dark times, you know they are truly your friend.

How many true friends do you have? Who are they?

July 23rd

"You don't stop laughing when you grow old, you grow old when you stop laughing."
- George Bernard Shaw

If we're lucky and we take care of ourselves, we face aging. We gain wisdom and experience. We go through all of the ups and downs that life has to offer us. But one thing we must never lose is our ability to laugh. Humor is one of life's most precious things. It helps us enjoy life's peculiar moments. It helps to comfort us and release all of our daily tensions. It helps to connect us to ironic ideas that make no sense. It helps to comfort us when we find ourselves down in the dumps. Taking life too seriously can only wear us down and break our spirit, but having a sense of humor, now that's the only way to take on what life has in store. Being playful and joyful releases natural endorphins that help the mind heal itself. It helps us melt away negativity and aggression. When we laugh with others, we connect with them. Those connections share a common belief that life is meant to be enjoyed. We can go after our dreams, but we must have fun during the journey!

What's funny in your life that can make you laugh?

July 24th

"People pretend not to like grapes when the vines are too high for them to reach."
-Marguerite de Navarre

I didn't want that anyways. She's so lucky. She must have slept her way to the top. She must have been born with it. These are all thoughts that victims play. They make excuses why someone has what they want but haven't received yet. It's not that they haven't received it yet, it's that they haven't achieved and earned it yet. No one has it all.No one is lucky. Sometimes they are in the right place at the right time, but there is no luck. There's awareness of opportunity. There's taking a risk on that opportunity. There's courage to think bigger. There's strength in meeting new people who are smarter and wealthier than you are. These are the things that make someone successful. It's not luck or circumstance. If you want to become successful, you can't depend on anyone else to give it to you and you certainly don't want to rely on luck. You must create a vision of what you want, meet the people that can help you get there, and take one action step at a time until you reach the finish line. Then you can have any grapes you want, no matter how high the vines are.

Are you still working on your dreams? What are you going to do today to get you one step closer?

July 25th

"The first key to wisdom is defined, of course, as frequent and assiduous questioning"
-Peter Abelard

How do we know something is fact? How do we know that we are wrong? How do we know that we are correct? How do we know something is possible? How do we know something isn't possible? We question. We criticize. We contemplate. We argue. We think of other ideas. We experiment. We prove. That's what science is, always questioning what facts are learned. That's what philosophy is, always questioning human existence and how we think and act in order to become better. That's what business and industry are, always thinking how to solve today's problems. We expand our personal knowledge by questioning our own routines and paradigms. We expand our culture and civilization by questioning the way society as a whole thinks and acts. Questioning is essential to growth and fulfillment. Questioning is the only way to move the bar a little further. Learning what works and what doesn't, but always questioning the results is what makes new things possible.

What are you questioning about your life today?

July 26th

"A journey of a thousand miles begins with a single step."
-Chinese Proverb

How do you eat an elephant? One bite at a time. It's the same with any big goal. It all starts with taking that first step. Sometimes it takes thousands of steps to get to your destination while other times it takes only a few. But the hardest part is getting started. The hardest part is making the decision that you need to head in a different direction and pivot to move in that new direction. Sometimes it can feel scary. Sometimes it can feel exciting. But no matter what emotion you have when taking that first step, be comforted in the fact that you're brave enough to start. You're brave enough to be aware that a change is needed and you're actually moving in the direction you need to move in order to make that change. Be proud of yourself because too many women stay in their comfort zones because it's safe and not many women go after what they truly want in their lives. But this isn't you. You're one of the few brave souls. You can do it. Don't be afraid to pivot or ask for help along the way. No question is a dumb question. Get the answers you need and keep moving towards your goals.

What's the first step you need to take today?

July 27th

"When you change your language from balancing to prioritizing, you see your choices more clearly and open the door to changing your destiny."
-Gary Keller, *The ONE Thing*

No one can have life balance. It just doesn't exist. We are constantly being pulled by our family, our career, and our friends. Good stuff happens. Bad stuff happens. And we're in the thick of it all. But that's what life is about. We can't do it all. We don't have enough time, energy, or money but we can prioritize what's important to us. If we focus our attention and resources on only doing the things that matter to us, we're eliminating about 90% of the things that clutter up our schedules and our focus. If our children and spouses are a priority, when we get home from work, we'll leave work at work and we'll make dinner and play a board game with them. If we need to get our project done, we'll eliminate any coworker's that want to chit chat and distract us from our main objective. If we focus on the one thing that's important to us at the moment, we can stop multitasking on multiple things and actually finish the one thing that can make a difference in our life. We will constantly be pulled in numerous directions, but if we keep our focus on the one outcome we want to accomplish, we'll find that we're an unstoppable force.

Where is your priority today?

July 28th

"Wasn't hitting bottom the thing you had to do to knock some sense into yourself? Wasn't hitting bottom the thing that showed you which way was up?"
– Rainbow Rowell, *Attachments*

We all have hit bottom at some point in our life. We had a failed relationship that devastated us. We got fired. We fell and broke something. We drank too much and had a hangover. We yelled at someone or said something we shouldn't and now we regret it. It happens. But we can't allow our mistakes to define us or be part of our identity. We must lace up our boots and try again. We must grow up and apologize when it's warranted. We must learn from our failures and try not to make them again. When we hit bottom, we are forced to look at ourselves and take responsibility for our actions. Only then, can we change them in the future. Only then can we grow and improve. Only then can we open our minds to new possibilities and outcomes.

What have you learned from hitting the bottom?

July 29th

"I suppose what I really am is restless. I want to go everywhere, see everything, do everything. I want to find something. Yes, that's it, I want to find something."
- Agatha Christie, Endless Night

We all can get bored. We all can get restless. Sometimes we find ourselves in dull, mundane routines that we want to snap out of. There's nothing wrong with wanting adventure and variety. That's what gives us meaning and fulfillment. That's what makes life interesting and exciting. That's how we learn and grow into better women. When we feel restless, we must listen to our instincts and figure out what we want to change and start moving in that direction. When we want to do something different, we must begin to open our minds to new ideas and concepts. We must start implementing these new actions into our lives. That will give us different results and give us the feeling of change and improvement that we're craving. When we want to change something, we can't be afraid of taking the first step in that direction. We must be brave and find what we're looking for. That's fulfillment. That's exciting. That's a great life.

What are you restless about today? What can you do about it?

July 30th

"Some women pray for their daughters to marry good husbands. I pray that my girls will find girlfriends half as loyal and true as the Ya-Yas."

-Rebecca Wells, *Divine Secrets of the Ya-Ya Sisterhood*

All women deserve to have good girlfriends. Women that will stand by you through thick and thin. Women that will support us. Women that love us unconditionally. Women that understand our highs and lows. Girlfriends are truly a remarkable thing. We all need someone to tell our inner demons to. We need others to celebrate our wins with and comfort us during our bad times. It's through these strong connections that we become whole. Our girlfriends help heal our wounds and lend a helping hand when we need them. They are truly a gift from God. Celebrate your girlfriends whenever you can!

Today's challenge: Text your girlfriends and plan a girls' night out.

July 31st

"The secret of happiness, you see, is not found in seeking more, but in developing the capacity to enjoy less."
-Socrates

Our society has depicted women as beautiful creatures. We need to look good at all times for us to be valuable in society. We need to have the right clothes, to marry into influence, to have perfect children, and to take care of the household. This is a lot of pressure for anyone. Wouldn't it be easier to have less? To live with less pressure? Do you have to keep up with the Joneses? To live more simply and efficiently? That's where Socrates was going. He questioned everything. If there was A, he wanted to know where B was and why A was A and B was B. Humans are conditioned to look for more, to progress, to improve. But there comes a time when it's okay to enjoy what you've done. What you've accomplished. What you have. It's okay to simplify your life and find happiness there. You don't have to look beautiful all day or depend on someone else for your worth or happiness in your life. You're enough.

What simple things in your life make you happy?

August

Hey Lady,

School will be starting for many kids. They will be adjusting their routines from fun, lazy summer days, to busy, chaotic scholastic periods. Now is a great time to transition our own time back to the vision of what we want in our lives. It's now time to focus on us. We need to get our thoughts focused on what's ahead. We need to get organized again. We need to make sure we get all of our activities done but still carve out some time to work on our personal goals. We can't allow the chaos of school and outside activities to stifle our progress towards reaching our own goals.

Prioritize your time and make sure that you focus on things that matter and let the rest go. You don't have to be a superwoman! You don't have to be perfect. You're a work of progress. Let that be enough!

It's time to focus!

August 1st

"Well-being is realized by small steps, but is truly no small thing."
- Zeno

Women tend to overestimate what they can accomplish in a short time frame. We love to multitask and think we have to accomplish everything all at once. That is a mistake that leaves us drained and unfulfilled. If we strive for progress over perfection, we can free ourselves of our obligations and burden of everyday life. Step by step, inch by inch, winning is a cinch. Right? How can you give your best self when you don't have time to improve yourself and you're constantly giving all your resources to everyone else? You need to give yourself grace and space to relax and so things for yourself. Then you can feel rested and recharged and ready for a new day to take on the tasks at hand. Give yourself a break and realize that not everything has to be accomplished right now. Small incremental steps can accomplish any big task. Persistence wears down resistance every day of the week.

What activity on your To-Do List can wait for another day? What will you do today to relax and recharge?

August 2nd

"With the new day comes new strength."
-Eleanor Roosevelt, *You Learn by Living*

Have you spent a night worrying about something? You didn't sleep and so the next day, you couldn't function to your fullest? Most people have done this. We've stayed up fighting with our spouse or worrying about something that *might* happen. Why waste our energy on fighting with someone or worrying about something that hasn't even happened? We need to take care of ourselves. We need to get our rest. We must rest our minds and our bodies so we can tackle the obstacles that come our way on a daily basis. If we're run down, we can't give our best efforts. If our minds are cluttered with worry and anxiety, we can't be creative and find the solutions we need. Tomorrow is a new day. Stop the fighting and worrying for tonight and drift off to sleep. Start again tomorrow when you have clarity and strength.

How can I turn off my worry and anxiety today so I can sleep well tonight?

August 3rd

"Be wiser than other people if you can; but do not tell them so."
-Dale Carnegie

Strong women don't talk about it, they show it. Intelligent women don't contemplate an idea, they try to manifest it into reality. Loving women don't keep their emotions to themselves, they love everyone around them. Be the woman you want to be. Show others what that means. Don't try to be her, do the things she would do. You can fake it until you make it, but never tell anyone of your intent as they may fill your head with doubt and anxiety. Instead, keep the vision in your mind and take the actions necessary to make that vision a reality. Others will try to keep you from changing, that's a normal thing. But it's their problem, not yours. They don't want you to outgrow them or leave them so they try to hold you back. Don't tell them what you want, show them what you want.

What do you want for your future? Be specific.

August 4th

If a person gave away your body to some passerby, you'd be furious. Yet you handover your mind to anyone who comes along, so they may abuse you, leaving it disturbed and troubled - have you no shame in that?

-Epictetus, *Enchiridion-28*

We are influenced by so many things. Social media. Our peers. The advertising and marketing world. Our families. Our communities. Our society norms. Some of us are easily swayed to think a certain way because tradition dictates it. Some of us believe that we have to live a certain way or have certain material goods to be popular or attractive. Some of us use every dollar and every ounce of energy to try to belong to a certain group thinking that they give us fulfillment. What we don't understand is that our minds are our most precious belongings. It's in our mind that the world that we want to live in first manifests. It's our creativity and our convictions that are most important. We shouldn't give our freedom to think independently and live the way we see fit to anyone. That includes free speech and free thought. Everyone is free to live as they choose without infringing on the freedoms of other people. Remember that when you're bombarded with society, marketing, and family messages and pressure. You are free to live your life as you choose. Choose wisely.

How can you cut out a bad influence today?

August 5th

"Believe and your belief will create the fact."
-William James

Manifesting our desires starts with a simple thought. That thought can then become an image in our mind on what goal we want to accomplish. We can imagine what our life would look like if we hit that target. If we lost that weight. If we met that person. If we finished that project. If we lived in that house. If we made that amount of money. If we can see other people living the lives that we desire, our subconscious mind can believe that it's possible and then start looking for ways to make that belief a reality in our own life. If you don't think you can do something, you certainly won't because you won't do what's necessary to accomplish that goal and you'll find every excuse in the book why it's not happening for you. Your success in life all starts in your mind and your soul. If you have convictions and beliefs on how you want to live, you'll find a way to make it happen. If you're not focused on what you want, you'll never create the path to get it. Imagining how your life can change is a simple, yet powerful way to kickstart the manifesting process.

What change can you believe you can accomplish?

August 6th

"If women are expected to do the same work as men, we must teach them the same things."

–Plato, *The Republic*

In America, women are free. We can have a career, a family, and our own direction without depending on someone else. But in order to have our own freedom, we must educate ourselves on how to get it. We must work on our careers. We must work on our networking. We must budget, save, and invest our money so our money accumulates and builds wealth over time. We must love and be available to our friends when they need us. We must build community and culture. We must act in the same way that men act in order to have the freedom that they enjoy. This doesn't mean that we can't work with men to create a mutual bond and relationships, but it means that we must start with our own lives first in order to be able to give our best to those that are around us.

What must we learn today that can help us become the best version of ourselves?

August 7th

"To continue to hold on to the old and inferior when the new and superior is at hand is to retard growth, and to this one cause may be traced many of the ills of man."

-Raymond Holliwell, *Working with the Law*

The safety zone. Our comfort zone. Our favorite pair of sweats. Our favorite coffee. When something becomes routine and habitual, then our curiosity of the world for discovering new things starts to wither. As children we see the world as a big exciting place. We play and imagine we're a superhero or a princess. We pretend to live in a different reality than we presently live in. But as we go through school, our creativity and imagination gets put on the back seat giving logic and rationality a dominant.We get comfortable in our routines because we can get predictable results. The problem is that we consistently get the same results. This tends to get boring over time. It retards our growth and progress as women. It keeps us from innovating and fixing the problems the world needs to be solved. We need to break out of our mundane, mediocre lives and look for fresh ideas and concepts that can spring life into our families and communities. Progress without growth and development doesn't exist. We must get rid of old ideas that no longer work and develop fresh, new perspectives that can help the world's issues.

What new ideas can you explore today?

August 8th

"If you reveal your secrets to the wind, you should not blame the wind for revealing them to the trees."

– Kahlil Gibran, *The Wanderer*

If we don't want others to know our thoughts, we should keep them to ourselves. As women, we communicate with others through speech. We like to talk about our feelings. We like to talk about our issues. We like to talk about other people. We are constantly expressing ourselves through our words. But it should be no surprise that our words can be repeated to other people. And sometimes those words may get distorted or rearranged in a negative way that can reflect badly on you. Our reputation is one of the most important things we can bring to the table. Our word that we will accomplish what we say we will. Our truth and the actions that are driven by our words matter. We can live our lives talking about our issues, or better yet, we can show the world what our feelings are through our actions.

What feelings can you change into action today?

August 9th

"There is nothing more unequal than the equal treatment of unequal people."
-Thomas Jefferson

We live in America. America is a free capitalistic nation that has some social programs that help people live normal lives. But we're not a socialist country. We are free to have the career that we want. We are free to own a business and make the products and services our communities need. Being successful in a career or having a successful business takes a lot of work and sacrifice. But that hard work and sacrifice has a price and that price is pretty high. Why should a woman that has simple skills be paid the same as a woman that has very complicated skills? She shouldn't. That's what a capitalistic society means. Your compensation is directly proportional to what you know, how well you know and show those skills, and the inability to replace you. It's difficult to be good at something. It's difficult to have a successful business. It's difficult to be at the top of the team. Because of the difficulty, you should be paid accordingly. Difficulty equals compensation.

How can you improve your compensation?

August 10th

"Your children will see what you're all about by how you live rather than what you say."
-Wayne Dyer

Children mimic everything they see. They want to learn. They want to improve. They want to grow up. This means they're watching us too. What we say and what we do directly influences the thoughts and actions of our children. If we tell them constantly that they can't do something because we ourselves don't believe that someone like us can do it, then they won't even attempt to succeed. If we're negative, they will be negative. If we lie, they will lie. If we blame others for our hardships and lot in life, they will grow up with the same attitude. If you want your children to be successful, we must not only tell them positive, supporting words, but we must show them that being successful is possible. That's what the wealthy do. They demonstrate what needs to be done and they teach their children to do the same things. To act the same way. To make the same types of decisions. They crack the code and they teach their children how to keep the success going.

What can you show your children about success today?

August 11th

"If you are depressed you are living in the past. If you are anxious you are living in the future. If you are at peace you are living in the present."
-Lao Tzu

We can't change the past, so why worry about it? We can't predict the future, so why worry about it? The only thing we can control and be aware of is this very moment. We can cause a certain result in the future if we take a certain action or make a certain decision right now. We can get healthier if we decide to make our next meal a healthy one. We can get healthier if we decide to go for a walk or go to the gym. We can decide to build wealth if we download a budget app and fill it in. We can decide to build wealth if we automate our investments. We can decide to be happy if we write down three things we're grateful for. We can be happy if we imagine what we want in our lives. The present is a gift that everyone has becaûse it can change the results we are getting in our lives. The time is now to make those changes that don't serve us. The time is now to create a plan to reach our goals. The time is now to take the first step towards success.

What is your plan for a change you want to make?

August 12th

"Success is not how many zeroes your bank account has. It's about making the most of the life you have."
- Suze Orman

Money won't make you happy, but it can be used to make life a lot easier. Money can help us travel, and live a debt free life. Money can be invested and help to support us when we're older. But unless we're happy and content in our lives today, we'll never be happy and content in our lives tomorrow. We must be grateful for what we've accomplished thus far. If we're just starting out, we must be grateful that we're young and have the energy and ambition necessary to move us towards our goals. We must be grateful for our loving families and spouses. We must be grateful for our health. We must relish in the fact that we live in a free nation and that we have the opportunities that not all women around the world have. Money and success won't make us happy, but it won't make us unhappy either if we use it as a tool of comfort and not envy.

How do you define success?

August 13th

"Smart people learn from everything and everyone, average people from their experiences, stupid people already have all the answers."
-Socrates

Have you ever met someone who doesn't listen and they know all of the answers? Have you ever been around a teenager? Have you ever gone to a seminar and noticed the room was full of CEO's and high executives who make a lot of money and are successful? Why would these people want to learn something new? Because they realize that there could be one simple idea that could transform their company into a leading competitor. Smart people are always learning. They are constantly questioning the status quo and the things that are believed as facts. That's how things change. That's how the world progresses and technology gets better. Smart people ask how they can improve their industries. Smart people ask how they can make a mark on their customers. Smart people ask how they can unleash their self-imposed limitations. If we only live by experience, we'll never get help from people who are winning at what we want to do. If we think we know all of the answers, we'll never improve our situations and we'll continue to get the same results year after year. Never be afraid to be the dumbest person in the room, you'll definitely learn something new.

Who can you learn from today?

August 14th

"It is not the length of life, but the depth."
- Ralph Waldo Emerson

Too many of us live on the surface. We spend our time doing simple mundane things, never accomplishing anything worthwhile. We often have many friends who are acquaintances but not many true friends. We earn the average wage, live in an average neighborhood, and have the average amount of things without earning to our potential. We live our lives by our habits and daily routines, never venturing out of our safety zones which give us the results we don't necessarily want, but accept. Why do we live like this? Why don't we kick things up a notch? Bring in some adventure in our lives? Most of us want a better life, but we're either too afraid or too lazy to go get it. Today is a great day to stop the madness and raise our standards for our lives and the people we surround ourselves with. Today is a great day to think bigger and better. Today is a great day to make a plan of attack and start moving towards our goals. Let's get in shape! Let's have some adventure! Let's make more money! Today is a great day to break the shackles that have been keeping us down.

How can you live life with more vigor and determination?

August 15th

"Education is teaching our children to desire the right things."
-Plato

What habits are you teaching your children? Manners? Wisdom? Health? Finances? Children need to master the basics of life and they need to be surrounded by good influences. If you don't have your life together, how do you expect them to grow up succeeding? Living in debt because you buy compulsively is not a good example. Being grossly overweight and eating nothing but junk food is not a good example. Being obsessed about being the best and pushing your children into activities and programs they're not interested in pursuing is not a good example. Children need good examples of love, health, community, God, and wealth.

Are you surrounding your children with good examples and giving them the right education? What are they?

August 16th

"When you struggle with your partner, you are struggling with yourself. Every fault you see in them touches a denied weakness in yourself."
- Deepak Chopra

We see *their* clutter. We see *their* dirty socks. We see *their* messes. *They* snore. *Their* breath smells. They make us mad. No one said it was easy living with another human. But sometimes we forget that *we* snore too much. *Our* breath smells. *We* do things that make them mad. *We* get messy. *We* throw our dirty clothes on the floor. It's far easier to just love our partners than it is to find fault with them. We're all human. We all have faults. None of us are perfect. Yet, sometimes we forget that fact and act like we're Mother Superior. Give your partner the benefit of the doubt and love them where they are. They are trying their best, even if it's not up to our high standards.

What struggles are you having with your partner?

August 17th

"Rational thought, to be effective in changing belief and behavior, must be accompanied by deep feeling and desire."
- Dr. Maxwell Maltz, *Psycho-Cybernetics*

In order to change something about our lives, we need to give something up. This could be a certain thought or belief. This could be a group of people we hang out with. This could also mean a habit that we have. We already know how to fix our problems, yet we still have them. Why? Most of the time it's because we don't really want to make the changes. *It would be nice to be like her. It would be awesome if I had that. It would be great if I looked like that.* Thinking and wishing for a certain outcome doesn't make it come true. We must throw in the knowledge of *how* with the action of *now* to start creating and maintaining the changes we desperately desire. Thinking and doing are two different concepts.

What change do you want to start today?

August 18th

"We are what we repeatedly do. Excellence, then, is not an act, but a habit."
-Aristotle

Thoughts turn into actions. What we spend our time doing every day defines us, and gives us part of our identity. If we work out every day, then we're a healthy person. If we stick to our budget and spend our money wisely, we are frugal. If we invest our money, then we are wealthy. If we question our current reality, we are growing. If we constantly work on our goals, we are ambitious. If we spend time with our spouse, we have a great relationship. If we do things with our kids, we are great mothers. Whatever actions you take, give you the results you're experiencing. If you want to experience different results, you must think differently and take different actions. It's not more difficult than that. You become what you do every day. If you want to change your outcome, change the path you're taking.

Are your habits creating a good identity?

August 19th

"One cannot step twice in the same river."
-Heraclitus

We are constantly changing. Our thoughts. Our beliefs. Our actions. If you look back on your life, are you the same person you were last year, five years, or ten years ago? Of course not! We've lived through a lot of life's experiences since then. We've conquered fears. We've gained insight and wisdom. We've succeeded and failed. We've grown as women. When we're faced with the same situation as we've dealt with in the past, we never act the same way. We're always evolving and improving. We can never go back. We can only move forward. Hopefully we're learning along the way and becoming better women. Hopefully we're using our talents and skills and leaving an impact on our families, our communities, and our careers. Hopefully we're realizing that every step we take makes new ripples that change the outcomes we experience. We can never go back. We can only move forward. Don't live in the past, take the experiences you've had and apply the wisdom you've learned to make the next round of decisions better and more fulfilling.

What problem have you solved better today than in the past?

August 20th

"If you don't find a way to make money while you sleep, you will work until you die."
- Warren Buffett

All of us spend a good part of our day working for money. We spend a lot of time and energy doing things for other people in order to earn our dollars. But what if there was a way to have our money work for us without doing anything? Is that even possible? Yes it is! It's called passive investing. We invest our money in the stock market whose companies make products and services for other people to use. These companies use their profits and reward us with dividends and higher stock prices. We can also invest our money in a side hustle that can earn us extra income without spending a lot of time. Maybe it's selling supplements or cosmetics where we earn money on the refills. We can also invest in real estate where our customers pay our mortgage and the extra cash flow that goes right into our pockets. Many of these ideas we buy once, and never have to revisit again until it's time to sell or improve our position. We can then repeat these types of purchases on and on until we make more money passively than when we work for it. That's true financial freedom.

What investments can you make money while you sleep?

August 21st

"Let food be thy medicine and medicine be thy food."
- Hippocrates

Americans are always obsessed with the newest diets. Adkins. Mediterranean. Keto. Paleo. Weight Watchers. Jenny Craig. Intermittent Fasting. One Meal a Day. The list goes on and on. But eating is really simple. Knowing what your body needs is instinctual. We need energy. That can come from simple and complex carbohydrates and fats. We need to repair and build new tissues, muscles, and bones. That can come from proteins and collagen. There's nothing our body needs that comes from a box. It's that simple. So when we do our shopping, we must think about giving our body what it needs in order to function at its best. That's fruits, vegetables, and meat. Anything you can get on the outside isles of your grocery store are what your body needs. When you do that, you're allowing your body to move and repair itself properly.

What's on the menu today?

August 22nd

"One beam, no matter how big, cannot support an entire house on its own."
-Chinese Proverb

No one can do everything. But as women, we bear the weight of being the support beam for our families, our careers, and our friends. We listen. We cook. We love others. We support others. We work. We help others. We do this each and every day and wonder why sometimes we start to crack and break down. What we don't realize is that we don't have to do it alone. They say it takes a village to raise a child, and this is so so true. This can also mean that we don't have to do anything alone. We are a community of women that are living the same lives as those around us all over the world and it is our duty to help support one another. When we help our friends and families, we are showing our love and our strength. But it also shows our love and our strength when we ask for help from those same people. Don't be too proud to ask for help. It will make things go faster and easier if we have help to conquer the tasks at hand. Support your community of women and allow them to support you and together we can make this world a better place to live in.

How can you help build a better community of women?

August 23rd

"The things which are most important don't always scream the loudest."
-Bob Hawke

Some days fly by fast while others creep at a snail's pace. Sometimes we work on things that matter while other times we stay busy without doing anything that gives us desired results. We can easily get distracted, disorganized, and off track. It takes a lot of work and discipline to stay on track and work effectively and efficiently on things that matter to us. At work, we need to prioritize our time and work effectively and efficiently at getting our projects done and creating production. At home, we need to prioritize our time and get the chores done, have great sex with our spouse, and spend time with our children. Some days, that's a tall order. But it is possible to get the big things done, we just have to give it our full attention and not allow other things to kick us off course.

What are you focusing on today?

August 24th

"Nobody who ever gave his best regretted it."
-George Halas

What would the world look like if everyone gave their best? Would there be war? Would there be poverty? Would there be hate and suffering? Hopefully not. Why do we spend our days doing things halfway? Are we acting this way because we feel pressured to do it all? Are we getting ourselves into situations that we don't want to be in because of other people's expectations of us? Are we lacking the energy, creativity, and drive to give our best on a continuous basis? It's possible. Is there any way to stop this madness? Yes! An easy way to give our best to our projects is to only focus on one thing at a time. If it's doing laundry, focus on only doing laundry. That way everything gets cleaned, folded, and hung up properly. If it's a project at work, then we need to get rid of all the distractions and problems that come up every day and only focus on the things that are necessary to get that project done to the best of our ability. If we're having trouble in our marriage, we need to focus our best energy on loving our spouse and making things right. When we focus our attention on one thing at a time, we can give our best attempt at that thing. Wouldn't that be a good thing? To give our best at everything every day?

How can you be your best today?

August 25th

"Those who look behind will never see beyond."
–Sherry K. White, *Walking in the Father's Riches: The Prosperity of Sonship*

The past is the past. We can't change it. What we need to focus on is the present moment. What can we change right now? What actions can we take right now? What can we learn right now? Who do we need to meet today that could help us achieve our goals? We all make mistakes. We all say things we shouldn't. We all have regrets. But all of those things are in the past. What kind of woman do you want to be today? Today is the perfect day to start living the way you want to live. Today is a great day to start building the future you want to see. Today you can set priorities. Today you can eat a healthy meal. Today you can exercise. Today you can create a budget. Today you can invest some money. Today you can call your mom and tell her you love her. Today you can have great sex with your partner. Today you can color with your kids. What's most important to you? Stop living in the past and start living in the present.

What's the plan for today?

August 26th

"The key is for you to discover what you love to do, what you were created to do, and then do it for the people around you with love. That is the abundant life, dear girl, no matter where in the world you live."
– Robin Jones Gunn, *Finally and Forever*

Everyone has a talent. Everyone is unique. Everyone has a purpose. Do you know what it is? Do you know what you're good at? If you do, are you sharing it with the world? Women are always comparing themselves with other women and focusing on their weaknesses. That's a waste of time. Instead of focusing on our weaknesses, we should be focusing on our strengths. We can accomplish so much more in our lives when we focus our attention on our strengths. Life is easier. It takes less effort and energy when we're doing things we love and come easily to us. We're in a better mood. There's less struggle. We're more positive. We exude confidence when we're positive and others can feel it. It's not fair to our families, our communities, and our offices when we're not playing to our abilities.

What are your strengths?

August 27th

"If we couldn't laugh we would all go insane."
- Robert Frost

Life can get pretty serious. It can drain our energy and our ambition. It can challenge our beliefs and it can harden our spirit. On the other hand, it can energize us and drive us beyond our limitations. It can also awaken our creativity and strengthen our love for one another. That's what makes living our best lives so fun and exciting. We're waking up each day looking around the next corner for new adventures and new ideas to explore. A great way to live life is through the senses of humor. With laughter we lighten the situation. With laughter we sugar coat the truth. With laughter we can set aside our differences and enjoy the silly moments together. Never be afraid to laugh at a situation. It can make everyone feel a little better when you can find humor in the moment. Watch a comedy. Get out your old yearbook. Dance and sing to your favorite song with your kids. Have a drink with your girlfriends and remember your college shenanigans. With a little humor, anything in life is worth enduring.

What makes you laugh? Spend some time today having fun.

August 28th

"He longed for cleanliness and tidiness: it was hard to find peace in the middle of disorder."
-Robin Hobb, *City of Dragons*

It's difficult to live in constant chaos. You can't find your phone. You can't find your keys. Your child's homework is missing. You come home to a house that's full of stuff that's out of place. That's no way to live! Our lives are meant to have some kind of order. Some kind of reasoning. Some kind of structure. Having a clean house can bring harmony to your life. Does your closet look like a disaster zone or are the clothes neatly hung up and folded? Can you see your kitchen counters or are they the catch-all for all your bills and backpacks?Are your drawers stuffed with clutter and your desk full of wrappers and garbage? If so, it's time for a wake up call and time for a cleaning day. It's time to get rid of the clutter and organize the stuff you keep. It's time to dust, wipe, and clean your house so that you're proud to have people over. It's time to put your house in order so that your life can follow. When your house is clean, your mind can relax and free itself from all the turmoil.

What can you clean and organize today?

August 29th

"If there's a single lesson that life teaches us, it's that wishing doesn't make it so."
– Lev Grossman, *The Magicians*

We can't wish for something to happen. We coulda, shoulda, and woulda our lives away. We dream of better times and lives that are filled with happiness and wealth. But happiness and wealth aren't created out of thin air. They need to be strategized. They need to be sculpted. They need to be supported and maintained. Nothing in life is free. Nothing in life is given to us. If we want it, we must go out and get it. We must be vulnerable to others. We must be driven to learn new things. We must risk our comfort for something different and better. We can't wait for something to happen *to* us, we must go out and make it happen *for* us. We must live our lives with purpose and vigor. Life is short and if we don't take the opportunities that present themselves, we're likely to waste it. Time is precious and we must spend it living the lives that we want instead of dreaming what it could be.

What are you going to make happen today?

August 30th

"Sometimes, the simple things are more fun and meaningful than all the banquets in the world."
– E.A. Bucchianeri, *Brushstrokes of a Gadfly*

There's something to be said about living the simple life. We are inundated with thousands of marketing messages every day leading us to believe that we need more. We need their products to make ourselves more beautiful. We need their products to keep up with our neighbors. We need their products to make us feel worthy. But again, we don't need their products to make us live a great life. Most good things in life are simple. Holding hands with your lover. Hugging your child. A capsule wardrobe where everything matches. A calendar with very few appointments. A bubble bath. Chocolate. Great sex. A funny joke. Things that release endorphins and make us feel good throughout the day. Living without an agenda and appreciating what you already have is the kind of life that can make you happy and fulfilled. Try it.

What are some simple things that you love? How can you bring more of them into your life?

August 31st

"The single most powerful element of youth is that you don't have the life experiences to know what can't be done."

– Adam Braun, *The Promise of a Pencil: How an Ordinary Person Can Create Extraordinary Change*

As we experience life, we tend to pick up baggage. We have relationships that go bad. We fail. We hurt ourselves and we hurt other people. We start out so innocent and so open to new ideas. We constantly learn and challenge what we think is correct. We constantly redirect our path until we find what we're looking for. Sometimes we find it, and sometimes we don't. The older we get, we need to remember to step out of our routines and comfort zones once in a while. We need to remember how fun life can be if we take a chance. We need to remember that we can have anything we want if we work for it. Our failures don't define us unless we quit dreaming and working towards our goals. Curiosity, creativity, and courage can steer us away from danger and into an enlightened path. Removing our limits can make anything we want a possibility.

Close your eyes. What does your perfect day look like?

September

Hey Lady,

The crispness is in the air this month. It's Fall. The leaves will be starting to turn beautiful autumn colors and will soon fall to make way for the dead of winter. Now is a great time to start cleaning up for the cold weather. Sweep out the garage. Pull all the flowers and plants in the garden and cover the ground. It's also a great time to declutter inside too. Go through your summer outfits in your closet and if you didn't wear them this summer, it's probably a good time to declutter and donate them. Clean out the closet and make room for something new. Sandals, belts, ear rings, and other accessories can be sorted through.

What about your makeup drawer? Are there half-used bottles of lotions and potions in the bathroom? Combine what you can and get rid of the rest. You really don't need five tubes of mascara. One is enough. Go through the linen closet and get rid of old ripped sheets, pillows, blankets, and towels. No one needs that many linens! Get ready to hunker down for the winter with a neat closet and bathroom.

September 1st

"When you first rise in the morning tell yourself: I will encounter busybodies, ingrates, egomaniacs, Liars, the jealous, and the cranks. None can do me harm unless I choose."
- Marcus Aurelius, *Meditations 2.1.*

People suck. There's no other words. But that doesn't mean that we should allow them to spoil our day, make us feel bad about ourselves, or rob us of our freedom. There will be people that piss you off today. There will be people that won't listen to you. But there will also be people that praise you and love you. So should you give up hope to all humankind just because there's a few bad ones out there? Of course not. Only you can make yourself feel bad. It doesn't really matter what anyone else does or says to you. Only you can give them power over you. Only you can react in a way that doesn't serve you. Why do you even care what the other person says or does? Do you even have to get involved? Allow people to act and feel the way they want to and keep yourself on track to having a good day. If they cut you off in traffic, don't get pissed, instead just think to yourself that maybe they are having a bad day and need to get to their destination faster than you do. If someone says something mean to you, take your time and respond logically or answer indifferently and not allow their words to sink into your consciousness. Start your day knowing that challenging things and people will come your way. Expect it and prepare for it so that when and if it does happen, you're ready to flourish and triumph.

Can you be cool today when someone or something gets under your skin?

September 2nd

"The quality of your life is in direct proportion to the amount of uncertainty you can comfortably live with.
-Tony Robbins, *UPW*

We as women want security in our lives. What we don't realize is that nothing is certain. Not our health. Not our day. Not the outside world. The only thing that is certain is that things are constantly changing. Some things for the good and some things for the not so good. But how can we respond positively to things and issues that come up in our lives? How do we cope when tragedy happens? Do we allow it to define us or do we allow it to transform us into something better? Billionaires don't become rich because everything they do works out. They become wealthy because they have the creativity to solve the problems that they encounter. They tend to fail quickly and bounce back even quicker. They constantly look for improvement and change and try to solve huge problems that no one else wants to touch. They turn uncertainty into certainty through hard work, creativity, and perseverance. You don't have to have a billion dollars to lead a rich life. You must embrace change and uncertainty and use the skills and the personality that you have to shape it into a personal victory.

How can you embrace something that's uncertain today and turn it into a win for yourself and your family? What uncertainty is in your control?

September 3rd

"You'd be surprised at the things that look great on the outside but are dysfunctional on the inside. Be sure to function as good as you look."
-T.D. Jakes

You may look at another woman and think, "She's got it made. Look at how perfect her life is. She is beautiful. She has a great husband and perfect children." But as we know, nothing is on the inside what appears on the outside. You never know what's going on behind closed doors. That perfect woman may be struggling with depression. One of her kids may be on drugs. Her marriage may be hanging by a thread. Instagram photos never capture what someone's true life is. It only captures that instant when everything looks peachy keen. But we all know that life has its ups and downs. That's why comparing ourselves to others isn't fair. We may think that someone has a perfect life, but if we walk in their shoes for a day, we may find that things aren't as wonderful as they seem on the outside. There's always struggles and challenges. If you're struggling with something, ask for help and get it fixed. When your outside reflects your inside, you can truly be happy. Until then, you will constantly be looking for something else.

What things are you struggling with? What steps can you take today to solve them?

September 4th

"Be present in all things and thankful for all things."
-Maya Angelou

Gratitude is definitely an attitude. A way of looking at life. When we dwell on the things that we've accomplished, the love we have in our lives, and our health, we can open ourselves to all of the wonderful possibilities that The Universe has in store for us. We must feel open and willing to experience it. In order to be open, we must be aware of how lucky we are. We must feel thankful for the time in history that we are living. We must feel grateful that we are free to express our ideas and create the lives that we want to live. We are truly blessed. We are not being raped of our dignity and our souls. We are not being beaten and degraded because we expressed our ideas. We are free. Take a moment and truly thank God for creating the wonderful you and for all you have surrounded yourself with. Giving thanks will set you free from the worries and anxiety that daily life can inflict upon your mind.

Take some time right now and write down 3 things you're grateful for today.

September 5th

"No man has the right to be an amateur in the matter of physical training. It is a shame for a man to grow old without seeing the beauty and strength of which his body is capable."
- Socrates

Most of us get out of shape. Even the ex-athletes get a little pudgy over time if they don't consistently work at it. Our bodies adapt very easily to their environments. If they're stressed, they have flight or fight hormones that are produced to help in their survival. We have metabolisms that break down the food we eat so our body can use it. What are we doing to our bodies to keep it healthy? Are we feeding it what it needs? Are we building it and sculpting it so it works at its optimum level? Do we push our physical limits on a daily basis? If not, why? Why aren't we building goddess bodies? Most men love the shapes of our bodies. Why not give them the best bodies we can have? We can live a long and healthy life, void of medications and medical treatment if we allow our bodies to work *for* us instead of *against* us. But it starts today.

How are you treating your body? What one thing can you start today to begin building your goddess body?

September 6th

"The important thing is not to stop questioning. Curiosity has its own reason for existing."
-Albert Einstein

If we knew everything, we'd be wealthy, healthy, and ultimately successful. But we're not. We need to continue to grow and improve our skills. Upgrade our environment. Expand our network. It's a never ending process through the course of our life. Do you remember when you were a kid? Everything was so new and fresh. We constantly used our imaginations and asked questions about everything. What changed? As we go through life, we should continue questioning everything. Even religion. Even political views. That's the only way to truly understand the world and do our little bit to be part of it.

What new thing or idea will you explore today?

September 7th

"The eye sees only what the mind is prepared to comprehend."
- Robertson Davies, *Tempest-Tost*

Our perceptions rule the way we see our world. If you are told to see brown in the room, your mind is triggered to see only brown things. But aren't there other colors in the room? Of course. Even if you're in a forest, there's other colors of bugs and plants surrounding you. But if you trigger a certain thought in your mind, you'll always see your world through that perspective. Identity and beliefs shape our perceptions. If we think we're fat, we'll always see ourselves as fat. If we see ourselves as ugly, we'll always see ourselves that way and we'll never try to improve ourselves. Our minds must be open in order to improve and grow. We need to explore and invite different opinions into our lives. We need to be around different people and expand our networks. Only then can our eyes see our world more clearly.

What people, ideas, and things can you open your mind to today?

September 8th

"The past has no power over the present moment."
- Eckhart Tolle

Some people go through horrific circumstances. They're raped. They're tortured. They're in an awful crippling accident. They're abused emotionally. Some make it out alive while others don't. The ones that survive are the ones that don't equal their pasts to their futures. They take their past experiences and learn from them. They build upon them. They realize that they survived and they strive to live the rest of their lives doing something wonderful with it. To contribute and help others. To become successful. To find love and be happy. We can't live in our past if we're going to have a happy life. We must build upon it and never repeat the history that has gotten us where we are today.

What bad memories from your past can you let go of today?

September 9th

"Remember, failure is an event, not a person."
-Zig Ziglar

Everyone fails. That's the only way to learn. Successful people learn, fail, try something different, fail again, try something different again, and finally succeed. It's a never ending process. If you fail, it shouldn't make you feel bad. So what? You tried and it didn't work. Try again. Try something different. Find a way around the obstacle. Hire a coach. Improve your skills. Practice some more. Do it again until finally you find success. That's what champions do. That's what successful women do. They don't allow failure to define them and they certainly don't quit. They pivot and keep progressing. They work at it until they succeed. And then they start over with another adventure. Welcome to life, ladies. The successful ones fail as quickly as possible and move on.

What failure have you experienced lately? Did you quit or did you try again?

September 10th

"To desire is to expect, to expect is to achieve."
-Raymond Holliwell, *Working with the Law*

When we expect to achieve our goal, we align our thoughts and actions with the end target. We network with the people that can help us hit our goal. We take the actions necessary to hit our goal. We go around the obstacles that get in our way because we know that our target awaits us on the other side. We know that it's possible for us to achieve it and thus, we have an expectation to succeed. If we allow anxiety, worry, or fear to creep into our thoughts, we hinder our ability to think clearly and creatively which will be necessary to reach our goals. Being confident and demanding excellence of ourselves and our outcomes can help us achieve the life that we want to live.

What expectations do you have today?

September 11th

"There is a kind of beauty in imperfection."
-Conrad Hall

Mother Nature herself creates things that are not perfect. There are animals and flowers that aren't symmetrical, balanced, or equal. Yet, all of the things that she creates are beautiful in their own way. We must not judge ourselves as ugly, chubby, or short. We must embrace the fact that we are all Mother Nature's creatures and that we all are beautiful in our own right. We have a purpose on this Earth and we must find that purpose and exude our intentions with all of our actions. We should never strive to be perfect, but to progress as an imperfect woman and improve ourselves and our families with the experiences and wisdom we learn throughout our lives. That's what makes life beautiful. That's what makes us and our imperfections beautiful. Our uniqueness is what is special about us.

What are your imperfections?

September 12th

"Whatever relationships you have attracted in your life at this moment, are precisely the ones you need in your life at this moment. There is a hidden meaning behind all events, and this hidden meaning is serving your own evolution."
–Deepak Chopra

People that we meet are sometimes people that can help us grow and become better women. That's why it's so important to network and meet new people. You never know when you'll meet someone that will make an impactful difference in your life. Maybe that is a new mentor that can help you create wealth and prosperity. Maybe that is a new friend that you can consort and have fun with. Maybe that is a new lover that you can form a lasting relationship with that can turn into a family and legacy. Being open to new people and ideas can help form our future. They can help challenge and strengthen our beliefs and daily routines. They can help us create progress where we may have slumped.

Is there a club or networking opportunity you can attend today?

September 13th

"Can you accept the notion that once you change your internal state, you don't need the external world to provide you with a reason to feel joy, gratitude, appreciation, or any other elevated emotion?"
–Dr. Joe Dispenza, *Breaking the Habit of Being Yourself: How to Lose Your Mind and Create a New One*

No one can make us happy. Nothing we buy or achieve will make us happy. We must feel happiness now, today, with whatever state we are in. We must be grateful for what we've accomplished thus far. We must love our life. When we live in this state, realizing how lucky we are to be alive and to live in the time that we live, then we can exude happiness and contentment. If we're always worried, how can we feel joy? If we're always feeling lacking or unworthiness, how can we feel appreciation? If we are sad, how can we feel happiness? If we're angry and resentful, how can we feel love and helpfulness? We can't feel both ends of an emotion at the same time. We can choose to be positive and feel positive emotions as much as possible. It is our daily choice.

What positive emotions can you feel today?

September 14th

"Fearlessness is like a muscle. I know from my own life that the more I exercise it, the more natural it becomes to not let my fears run me."
-Arianna Huffington

Fear can mean "False Evidence Appearing Real. We all have it. We all face it on a daily basis. The difference between successful women and unsuccessful women is that successful women move forward anyways, whereas unsuccessful women stop dead in their tracks. The unsuccessful women allow their fears to get the best of them and halt their forward progress. Successful women keep moving forward, even though they're terrified inside. But they don't allow their fears to wither away their ambition and drive. The successful women go after their dreams no matter what negativity is going on in the back of their minds. We all have doubts. We all have hesitation. We all have peer pressure. But we must move past it all in order to manifest the life we truly want. It takes courage, mentoring, and extreme perseverance in order to make things happen. But in the end, we all can accomplish anything we set our minds to. We just need to get out of our safety zones and venture into the next adventure that awaits us.

What are you afraid of?

September 15th

"Ask for help. Not because you are weak, but because you want to remain strong."
-Les Brown

Through the ages, women have been viewed as the weaker gender. Even though we are physically weaker than men in many ways, we are mentally and emotionally superior. Why? Because women help each other. Women encourage each other. Women listen and support others that are struggling. It's in our DNA. We nurture. We love each other. We ask for help from others, not because we are weak, it's because we're courageous in wanting to improve something in our lives and we acknowledge the fact that someone else knows the answers that we seek. Improvement and living our best lives entail learning new things. It involves failing and trying again. That doesn't mean you are weak, that means you are courageous and you have a burning desire to improve and get stronger. Seek out mentors to help you in every area of your life that you want to improve.

Can you ask for help today?

September 16th

"Life is short, but there is always enough time for courtesy."
-Ralph Waldo Emerson

What happened to manners? America has become a rude and mannerless society. It's a shame. What happened to saying *please* and *thank you*? Why aren't you holding a door for me as I go into a store? Where's the respect for others? Social media has helped the younger generations become opinionated jerks. They think their opinions actually matter. Let's face it, they really don't. Instead of keeping our minds open to new ideas and opinions, we shut down and cancel anything that doesn't agree with our beliefs and ideas. What happened to free speech? Other cultures don't do this. They're respectful, especially to older people. They keep things formal and courteous to strangers. They respect authority. They work within their lane. They don't argue and don't demand respect where they haven't earned it. It's the way America acted in the 1950's. We need to get back to those days if there's any hope for our nation.

How can you show your manners today?

September 17th

"Too much attention to problems kills our faith in possibilities."
-Price Pritchett, *Firing Up Commitment During Organizational Change: A Handbook for Managers*

It won't work for me. I can't do that. People like me don't do things like that. These are all self-sabotaging and limiting thoughts. Yes, we need to focus on our problems, but we can't be engulfed by them. We can't allow them to hold us back from living the life we want. Instead of dwelling on the problem, we need to switch our focus and attention on finding the solutions to those problems. Not everyone has the same problems. Why can't we find the people that don't have the problem we do and find out what they do differently to eliminate that problem from their life? Having a mentor to show you the way cuts down on the time and energy you need to solve the problem. You don't have to figure it out and waste precious resources. Follow their lead and solve the problem with focused attention and action. Instead of saying, " I can't," say out loud, "How can I?" When you ask yourself this question, your subconscious mind starts looking for the answer. If you say you can't do something, you shut down your potential before you even get started.

How can you solve your problem today?

September 18th

"When intelligent people read, they ask themselves a simple question: What do I plan to do with this information?"
-Ryan Holiday, *Trust Me, I'm Lying: Confessions of a Media Manipulator*

Some people read fiction. Some people read nonfiction. Some people don't read at all. What we need to focus on is what we're trying to get out of the words in those books. If you're trying to escape from your mundane stressful life, then reading about a different world through fiction is a good way to spend your time. If you're trying to improve your mindset and learn how to do something to increase our wealth, then nonfiction is very useful. If you don't read at all, you must ask yourself if you're living the life you want. Are you healthy? Are you wealthy? Do you have great relationships? If not, there's a plethora of knowledge and wisdom that live inside of nonfiction books that are ready for you to absorb and implement in your own life. Most of the information can be accessed for free from your local library. Reading about past experiences from other people can help leapfrog success in your own life. It's amazing how little time it takes to transform your life from a few books on a certain subject.

What are you reading today? How are you going to use that information?

September 19th

"The first step in crafting the life you want is to get rid of everything you don't."
- Joshua Becker

We live cluttered lives. We buy too many things that we don't really need, so our house is a constant mess. We have too many activities on our calendars, so our time is never our own. We take on too many projects at work and spend our days in chaos. We're constantly stressed, tired, and wishing for a vacation. What if we could feel like we're on vacation every day without going anywhere? It's possible if we start to simplify our lives. If we get rid of the clutter, rid of the distractions and obligations, and rid of the constant chaos, we could live quietly and stress free. Wouldn't that be nice? It's possible but it takes a lot of discipline and work to get rid of all the cluttered areas of life. The question you need to ask yourself is do you really want it? If you want to live more simply and without stress and anxiety, start getting rid of things in your life that don't matter to you. This includes physical possessions, activities on your calendar, projects at work that someone else can do, and of course, people that aren't contributing to your life. When you find simplicity, you'll find peace.

What can you get rid of today to help you find peace?

September 20th

"He who asks is a fool for five minutes, but he who does not ask remains a fool forever."
-Chinese Proverb

Some people are afraid of asking questions. They don't want to feel foolish in front of other people. Yet, questions are the very thing that are responsible for the development of society as we know it. Breakthroughs in technology and science would never be possible if someone didn't question the status quo. What is believed to be facts are not necessarily true until they are proven to be so. People that live an average life do so because they don't ask how they can change their lives. They're too afraid to try and fail and their pride keeps them in their safety zone. Is that the way you want to live? If not, then it's time to start questioning everyone and everything that you know. Why? How? When? What? Who? These are all simple questions that you can ask to start to open your eyes to new ideas and possibilities that you can incorporate in your own life. If it's possible for someone else, it's possible for you. Don't be afraid to ask questions and start to change your beliefs and limitations you've formed in your own head. Don't be afraid to try and fail, it's all part of the learning method. It takes time to make a change and your change will be no different. Don't remain average. Ask others how you too can change your life and start living the life you've always dreamt of. It's possible for you!

What will you question today?

September 21st

"Multitasking is merely the opportunity to screw up more than one thing at a time."
-Steve Uzzell

All women think they need to be excellent multitaskers. We do laundry, play a game with the kids, and start dinner all within a matter of a few minutes when we get home from work. But do we need to do all of these things at the same time? No. Yes, the laundry needs to get done, but maybe we can start it after dinner. Yes, the kids need some attention, but maybe we can concentrate on dinner first, prepare a good nutritious meal for them, and then after we refuel our own body, we can start to take on other activities and give our attention to those that need us. It's possible to do one thing at a time. It's possible to say no and concentrate on the one thing that needs priority. We can choose what and who we give our attention to. We can decide what tasks need to be completed right now and which ones can wait. We don't have to do everything all at once. Isn't that wonderful? Don't you feel free? Don't you feel the weight off your shoulders? Get rid of the notion that you have to be a superwoman and concentrate on giving your best self to everyone and everything each and every time. Then you'll slow down and actually accomplish something.

How can you stop multitasking today?

September 22nd

"The effect of successful assertion on the audience is not taken to be belief, but commitment. It is not the intention of the speaker which matters in the first instance, but the social authority of his remark. It is not the speaker's intention which brings about the desired effect, but the social convention or practice governing his remark."

-Robert Brandom, *Asserting*

Assertion has been difficult for women to do in the past. To stand up for your opinions and your rights have oftentimes been stammered by cultural and social norms. Speaking your truth and standing up for yourself is of the utmost importance to live a happy and fulfilling life. Never allow anyone or anything to stifle your character.

What issue can you take a stance on today?

September 23rd

"Our wounds can so easily turn us into people we don't want to be, and we hardly see it happening. Protect your heart, love yourself, and be with people who love and care for you."
-Sue Fitzmaurice

It's easy to become cynical, critical, and pessimistic. Once we've been hurt, a small part of our heart, our innocence, and our nurturing nature can be hardened. Over time, the hurt can grow until it suffocates all the love that we want to have. Life isn't easy. People can be cruel. But that doesn't mean that we surrender our lives to circumstance or someone else's agenda. Surround yourself with people that love you. Surround yourself with positivity and optimism. Control yourself, your emotions, and your actions. Don't give the power of your life, your energy, and your identity to anyone. They belong only to you and only you can use them to their fullest. Everyone will get hurt. Everyone will go through bad times. But it's in those times that great women are born. It's in those times that the true spirit and strength of women come through for the world to see.

How can you protect your heart?

September 24th

"Always laugh when you can, it is cheap medicine."
-Lord Byron

Today is a great day to plan some fun. Grab a blanket and some food and go to the park for a picnic. What about a nice walk around the neighborhood with your son? You're working way too hard to not have something fun to look forward to. Maybe you can start planning an end-of-the-year vacation. Maybe you can get away for a weekend with your spouse. Sometimes it's fun to make plans. What about sending the kids out with your spouse while you soak in a nice bubble bath and listen to some nice jazz music while sipping on some wine. What about going to the store, stocking up on supplies, and spending the day painting your favorite scene. Whatever hobby or activity you enjoy, today is the day to enjoy it. Don't get bogged down with obligations today, you deserve a break.

What kind of fun are you going to have today?

September 25th

"Through discipline comes freedom."
-Aristotle

Discipline is difficult. People that seem to have it all, have extreme discipline. The professional athlete gets up at 5am to start their morning workout. They continuously work on the fundamentals of their sport. But all we see is their amazing catch to win the game. We don't see what they go through on a daily basis. When we're sleeping under the warm covers, they're out in the cold practicing. The same goes for those that have built companies and wealth. We only see what they have now, we don't see the years of struggle and hard work they put in to get their companies to the success that they are today. The discipline that these people have shown has rewarded them with wealth, health, and success. They put in the work in the beginning, and they've enjoyed the rewards in the end. That's what it takes to enjoy freedom. You sow the seeds, you tend to the garden, you pull the weeks, and then a couple of months later, you enjoy the fruits of your labor. And there's usually more fruit to enjoy than there was work that was put into it to start. Do the hard thing today to experience the easy fun things tomorrow.

What areas of your life do you need more discipline?

September 26th

"If you're reading this. Congratulations, you're alive. If that's not something to smile about, then I don't know what is."
-Chad Sugg, *Monsters Under Your Head*

Today is going to be a great day! Fall is here and the leaves are starting to turn color. The wind is starting to cool down and Mother Nature is starting to prepare for winter. Look in the mirror. What are you noticing? Is it time to dye my gray hair? Pluck your eyebrows? Lose a few pounds? Look at your calendar. Is it full of activities and meetings that aren't important to you? What about your house? Is it full of stuff that you don't really need or use but just gets in the way? Today is a great day to reset anything that doesn't matter to you. Today is a great day to tackle the chores and put your house in order. Today is a great day to move, feel the sunshine on your face, and let everyone around you know that you're a force to reckon with. Today truly is a great day to be alive!

What's on the agenda today?

September 27th

"If experience is the best teacher, there's nothing that comes close to the experience of life."
- Michael A. Singer, *The Untethered Soul: The Journey Beyond Yourself*

We need to live in order to learn. We need to explore in order to know what to avoid. We need to risk something in order to know if it was worth it or not. This is the only way we gain experience about life. We must take a chance. We must try and fail. We must love and lose. We must experience both sides of the coin. That's what we call a rich life. That's what makes life exciting. That's what gets us up in the morning, full of energy and wonder on what the day will bring. Don't live your life through the experience of others. Go out and live it for yourself. If you do, you'll never have regret or remorse. Life is too precious to spend it on the couch.

What will you experience today?

September 28th

"Things can be cleaned and replaced. Great moments cannot afford to be lost."
- Cindy Woodsmall, *The Bridge of Peace*

Now's the time for great sex. Yes, the chores can wait. Your partner is giving you the look, it's time to go for it and be spontaneous. Or maybe it's the time to relax and unwind from a long day at work. Maybe it's time to order some takeout and watch a movie. Or maybe it's time to play a board game with your children. Sometimes you need to relax. Sometimes you need to have some fun. It can't be all work and no play. Sometimes you must put off the obligations you have for the memories you can create with the ones you love. Time goes by so fast, today's a great day to enjoy it by doing something fun and relaxing. You deserve it.

What fun things do you have planned today?

September 29th

"Every game is winnable if you change your mind about what the prize should be and your perspective about the players at the table."
- Shannon L. Alder

Never be jealous of other women who are succeeding. Instead, observe what they're doing and start implementing the same actions in your own life. Don't hate the player, hate the game, right? You can be just like them if you put some effort and attention on it. Sometimes you may think it's impossible for you to succeed or achieve your lofty goal. You'll never know if you can do it, unless you try. Maybe it will take you longer, but who cares? Maybe you'll stumble and fail numerous times, who cares? Maybe you'll have to improve in many skill sets in order to achieve that goal, who cares? As long as you don't quit and you keep your eyes on the prize, anything you want to accomplish is yours for the taking. Once you've reached your milestone, reflect on what it took to get there, and figure out what your next move is. Maybe you'll continue improving, or maybe you'll find that you have enough and you just want to enjoy it. Either way, you've won!

Where is your focus today?

September 30th

"Listen to the whispers or soon you will be listening to the screams."
-Elisabeth Gilbert

We tend to let things go. The drip in the faucet. The pain in your right knee. Old bills that need shredded. But if we wait on these things, they just get worse. The whole faucet may need to be replaced instead of just a cheap washer. Your knee may need scoped because of the wear and tear that's gotten worse. The paperwork clutters your desk until you can't use it anymore. Letting things go only makes things pile up and get worse. Today is a great day to get your crap together and take care of business. Ask for help from coworkers, family, and friends. You don't have to do it alone! Apologize before the issue gets worse. Clear the clutter and clean up the mess. Focus your attention and energy today on getting rid of the little issues that are going on in your life.

What issues do you have to clear up today?

October

Hey Lady,

Have you been networking lately? Have opportunities been knocking at your door? If not, now is a great time to start talking to new people. Join a club or join a networking group. The year is winding down, but new opportunities are always available if you put yourself in the position to take them. This means getting out of your comfort zone and talking with others. Make new friends. You don't have to sell anyone anything. By building relationships with others, you set yourself up to be in the front of their consciousness when a problem arises. Maybe you can help your new acquaintance with your products or services.

But networking is not about selling others. It's about developing new alignments with others. You never know when you might find someone to hang out with during your kids' soccer games. You never know when you may find a new doctor or new project manager. Make sure you get out there and meet someone new.

October 1st

"My treasure lies in my friends ."
- Alexander the Great

Wealth does not come from money alone. Wealth is also from the people that you surround yourself with. Your family. Your friends. A great girlfriend is worth more than gold. She's there to listen, to encourage, and to stand by you no matter what happens. You don't need a large group of friends to feel rich. All you need is one great girlfriend that has your back no matter what obstacles come your way. Through the good and bad. Through the thick and thin. Someone to explore life's journey with and to create adventure. To laugh. To sing. To cry and to drink. Someone you can make memories with and share your inner thoughts and tribulations. That's a true girlfriend. That's someone that you can trust and journey through life with. Celebrate your close girlfriends this week and create new memories you will all remember.

Who do you need to call and what plans do you need to make?

October 2nd

"The children now love luxury; they have bad manners, contempt for authority; they show disrespect for elders and love chatter in place of exercise. Children are now tyrants, not the servants of their households. They no longer rise when elders enter the room. They contradict their parents, chatter before company, gobble up dainties at the table, cross their legs, and tyrannize their teachers."
-Socrates

If you're a parent, how are you raising your children? Do they have manners? Do they do chores? Do they value education? Do they practice moderation? Are they healthy? In order for our society to improve and continue to progress, we must teach the next generation about history and mistakes from the past. We must teach them how to be adults and take care of themselves. To not be a burden on society. To be healthy, wealthy, and wise. But we can't teach what we don't know. If we ourselves are not healthy, wealthy, and wise, how will we teach our children? We can't. So today, take some time to reflect on how your children act and create a plan on teaching them something new.

What can you teach your child today?

October 3rd

The number one rule is: my lover comes first. If you're in love, you put their feelings and needs before your own."
-Tony Robbins

If you've been in a relationship for a decade or more, you realize that this may not be true anymore. We all can get busy with our kids, our careers, and our activities. But where in our lives is our relationship? This is the person that you should be concentrating most on in your life. What makes them happy? What makes them angry? Focus on carving out some time each day to reconnect with your partner. With your lover. With your soulmate. Many times we lose our focus and make our children our priorities. This can mean that we wake up one day and our husbands leave us for their young secretary. Why? Because they didn't feel they were a priority in your life. Don't make that mistake. Make time to do fun things together. Date nights. Hot sex. A weekend away. Anything that can help bridge that gap that your partner might feel. Connect and rebuild the most important relationship in your life. Don't let outside circumstances and lack of attention spoil the life you've built.

What will you do today to rebuild your relationship with your partner and make them your number one priority?

October 4th

"The more you praise and celebrate your life, the more there is in life to celebrate."
- Oprah Winfrey

Life is too short not to have fun. We tend to only celebrate the holidays or special occasions. Why not celebrate the small wins? Every day we experience small victories. We finished a long project at work. We had a hard workout. We finished our kid's science project. No matter how small the win is, we should celebrate it. Eat a piece of chocolate. Drink a glass of wine. Do a little dance. Shout with joy. No matter what it is, we should celebrate it. Everyone needs encouragement and support. Why not show it by celebrating each step along the way? Each step is one step closer to the main goal. Why not enjoy the journey along the way and not just the destination?

What small wins can you celebrate today?

October 5th

"Rich people acquire assets. The poor and middle class acquire liabilities that they think are assets."

—Robert Kiyosaki, *Rich Dad Poor Dad*

Your house is not an asset. Even when you pay off the mortgage, you still owe property taxes and upkeep. It will forever be taking money out of your pocket. A true asset is something that puts money in your pocket. A rental property. An oil investment. A trading bot. Online programs. Books and song royalties. Things that you can create or buy once and can pay you month after month. That's a true asset. Wealthy people spend their money acquiring assets that pay them. Then they spend the cash flow on either more assets or to pay their bills. Cash flow dividends are taxed differently than your job income. It's a lot less. That's how the wealthy become wealthier and that kind of wealth takes specialized knowledge.

What knowledge do you need to learn to become wealthy?

What class or mentor do you need to sign up with?

October 6th

"If you can't do great things, do small things in a great way."
- Napoleon Hill

Be the best at whatever it is you're doing. If you stay home with the kids, be the best mom you can be. If you're a wife, be the best wife you can be. If you're a doctor, teacher, or engineer, be the best person with those skill sets as you can be. Most of us won't be famous, invent something that will change the world, or win a gold medal. But all of us have skills and talents that are unique to us. All of us can give our best. All of us can live to our potential no matter what that entails.

What small things can I do in a great way today?

October 7th

"Busy your mind with the concepts of harmony, health, peace, and good will, and wonders will happen in your life."

–Joseph Murphy, *The Power of Your Subconscious Mind*

Our thoughts help to shape our realities. If we're living in harmony, we are constantly going along with the ebbs and flows of our life. We don't get caught up on obstacles that get in our way, we find ways around them. If we're living healthy, we're challenging our bodies with exercise and giving it the raw ingredients it needs to perform optimally. If we're living in peace, we're constantly improving ourselves and becoming aware of our strengths and weaknesses. If we're living with good will, we're helping others and being a good neighbor. If we're living in wonder, we're constantly questioning the status quo and trying to find what's true and what's not. All of these things help you to make the most of your life.

Which concept above do you need to focus more attention on?

October 8th

"We have three major ways of handling feelings: suppression, expression, and escape."

—David R. Hawkins, *Letting Go: The Pathway of Surrender*

We all have different ways we deal with emotions. If we suppress them, we hide them deep down within us. That can lead to depression and undo anxiety. If we let out our emotions anytime we have them, we can't think logically and can end up making our situations worse. If we try to ignore and escape our feelings, we tend to keep running and never deal with the cause of our feelings. None of these situations help us to improve and grow as women. We need to think of our feelings as a mental response that can make our body act in peculiar ways. We cry. We laugh. We shout. We run. It's quite normal and okay to have the feelings we have, but we must learn to control them so they don't control us.

How do you handle your feelings?

October 9th

"If you place your head in a lion's mouth, then you cannot complain one day if he happens to bite it off."
-Agatha Christie

We all can find ourselves in a bad situation. In a lie. In trouble. But there's always a way to get out of that situation by not getting in it in the first place. Our word is our integrity. If you can't be trusted, then you will never have any support and we all need support and love in our life. Don't put yourself in a compromising situation. Even if it's for a loved one. Even if it's for a friend. Even if it's for money because in the end, you'll be the one holding the bag and will be punished for it. Never put your head in the lion's mouth.

What situations can you avoid getting into trouble with?

October 10th

"Every strike brings me closer to the next home run."
– Babe Ruth

Obstacles. Failure. Setbacks. Defeat. Collapse. We all experience them. But the successful women are the ones that brush themselves off and try again. They don't give up. They do whatever they need to do to learn how to push through their obstacles. They don't allow their negative emotions to overtake their beliefs and confidence that they can succeed. Everything in life is mind over matter. Every step you take is one step closer to your goal. You may need to take 10, 100, or even 1,000 steps in order to achieve it, but as long as you take each step, you're closer and closer to victory and achievement.

What step can you take today that gets you closer to your goal?

October 11th

"Trust yourself. You know more than you think you do."
—Benjamin Spock

We all have doubts. We all worry that what we're doing is wrong. If we have children, we may think that our decisions will scar them for life. And sometimes they will, but that doesn't mean that we give up. We must do the best we can with the tools that we have. We must feel confident that the decisions we make today are good enough. We may face consequences for them in the future, but that's okay. We can deal with them when they arrive, if they arrive. In the meantime, we must face today with excitement and vigor. We must face all obstacles with confidence and grace. When we do this, we can build experiences that can serve us in the future.

How can you trust yourself more?

October 12th

"You can make money or you can make excuses but you can't make both."
- Grant Cardone

How many times have we blamed other people or circumstances for our lack of money? Someone else got the promotion over you. Something happened and you had to fix your car with a credit card. You didn't have anything saved up so you borrowed money to go to school and now you're thousands of dollars in debt. Money problems usually are associated with a lot of excuses. Today is the perfect time to make a change. Today is a great day to get your finances in order. It will take some time to get them fixed, but it's not impossible no matter how terrible they are. Today is a great day to take out a sheet of paper or open a spreadsheet and create a budget. Today is a great day to think about what you'd like to see in our bank account and investments and start telling your money what to do. It's time to stop the excuses and start taking action.

How are you going to fix your money today?

October 13th

"Adventure is worthwhile in itself."
-Amelia Earhart

Most of us love to live in our comfort zones. We don't want to rock the boat too much. But where is the fun in that? Where's the adventure? Where's the uncertainty? Where's the variety? Sometimes life will throw us an opportunity that can totally redirect our path. We must be ready to take it. We must ready ourselves to be creative and think out of the box in order to improve things in the world. Without adventure, we'd still be living in a cave and bearing children every year. Our lives can become mundane with chores, children, careers, and communities. Why not meet someone new today? Why not join a new group? Why not take a new project that's out of your department? Why not venture out into the world and discover new and challenging things? Only then can we grow and improve our lives. Only then can we say that we lived our lives and didn't just take up space until we die.

What adventures can you have today?

October 14th

"If you want to know what a man's like, take a good look at how he treats his inferiors, not his equals."
– J.K. Rowling, *Harry Potter and the Goblet of Fire*

This is called humility. We are all human. We are all women. Just because someone has less money or status than we do, doesn't mean we are superior. They just have different circumstances. That doesn't mean that we treat them differently. The Golden Rule applies here- treat someone like you want to be treated. Would you treat your mom like that? Would you want to be yelled at like this? Would you like to be ridiculed or made fun of? Women can certainly gossip and act cady. It's shallow and self righteous. That doesn't mean it's the right thing to do. Be nice to everyone and you will earn the respect that you seek without taking it away from someone else.

How can you show kindness today?

October 15th

"Life is not easy for any of us. But what of that? We must have perseverance and above all confidence in ourselves. We must believe that we are gifted for something and that this thing must be attained."
-Marie Curie

Everyone is going through something. It may be big, it may be small, but we're all dealing with issues on a daily basis. This forces us to give grace to others. We should give them the benefit of the doubt as much as possible. If someone cuts us off on the road, they must be in a hurry for something important. If someone yells at us, they are probably frustrated about something else and not really with us. Grace helps us rise above the petty issues and continue to strive for the best in our lives. Petty arguments and situations only prevent us from moving closer to our goals. Don't allow other people's issues to spoil our moods and our positive outlook. Remember, everyone has problems they're dealing with. Focus on what we can control and brush off the other stuff.

How can you show grace today?

October 16th

"Reserve your right to think, for even to think wrongly is better than to not think at all."
-Hypatia

Everyone has the right to create an opinion. Or no opinion at all. Everyone has the right to gather all the facts and form an educated guess. It could take time. It could take several attempts to get things right. That's what science is about. That's what society is about. That's what relationships are about. Trial and error. Working to get things right. Working for progress and improvement. Cooperation. Integrity. We need to take the emotion out of the situation and think about it logically and rationally. That's when progress can be made. That's when change occurs. Being aware of issues that need to be changed and having the level headed approach to make the changes needed.

What are you thinking about today?

October 17th

"Every time you borrow money, you're robbing your future self."
-Nathan W. Morris

There are trillions and trillions of dollars that have been borrowed from credit card companies and also for student loans. Car, boats, and mortgage payments take our paychecks every single month. What would it feel like to not owe anyone anything? Total freedom. We think that we can afford something because we can afford the payment, but in reality, if we can't afford to buy it now, we can't really afford it later. Our society has crippled itself with debt payments. When we get our paychecks, we realize that it goes out just as fast as it comes in and we only have a few things to show for it and it doesn't allow us to plan for our future. Most of the time there's no money left over to save for a rainy day. And if we can't save any money because there's no money left, we certainly can't invest any money to work for us and multiply. This enslaves us and makes us dependent on our jobs and our energy to continue to work and bring in money to pay for our debts. What if we can turn this around? We can, if we can learn to be disciplined, budget our money, and practice delayed gratification. When we can delay our purchases in lieu of saving and investing, then we can enjoy the fruits of our labor. But for now, we must break the debt chains that are holding us down and never strap ourselves with debt again in order to live our lives like we want.

What's your plan for getting out of debt?

October 18th

"The First wealth is health."
- Ralph Waldo Emerson

If we don't have our health, we don't have much. There's so many people who are overweight, taking lots of medications, and who struggle to function normally on a daily basis. Diabetes, cardiovascular disease, cancer, and Alzheimer's are some of the main diseases that people face. We must focus our attention on daily fitness and nutrition in order to keep our body moving and functioning in a normal capacity. Most of the conditions we face that are due to our eating habits can be eliminated if we take control of our eating habits. If we're shopping on the outside of the grocery stores for the fresh fruits, vegetables, and meats, we can give our bodies the necessary ingredients to fight off disease and function normally. No one can be happy living in a body that doesn't feel good. If your joints hurt, if you can't bend over to tie your shoes, if you're winded after climbing one floor of steps, now is the time to get ahold of your true wealth, which is your body.

What can you do today to give your body what it needs?

October 19th

"It is not the knowing that is difficult, but the doing."
-Chinese Proverb

We all go to school for many many years. We are constantly learning how to do things. We are constantly learning what we should do and we shouldn't. But how many things are we not doing? How many things are we getting wrong even though we know better? How many times are we handling things incorrectly even though we know what to do? The answer is probably too high to count. We all know what it takes to budget, save, and invest to create wealth. It's common sense. We all know what it takes to exercise and eat properly to maintain a healthy and strong body. It's common sense. We all know what a good relationship is. It's common sense. We all know how to be a good leader and build a successful career and business. It's common sense. So why isn't everyone succeeding? Why isn't everyone healthy? Why isn't everyone rolling in wealth? It's because we *know* what to do, we just don't *do* it! Knowing something and doing something are two different things. We are fearful that we will fail. We are scared of what others will think of us. We are afraid to start. We are afraid of getting hurt. We are afraid of getting out of our comfort zones and trying something new and different. It's all about fear. But in order to live the life we know how to live, we must face our fears and get over them and start living for ourselves.

What are you going to *do* today that you know you *should* be doing?

October 20th

"Focus is a matter of deciding what things you're not going to do."
-John Carmack

'No' is a great word. As women, we need to use it more often. For some reason, we get it in our minds that we have to do everything. We have to be the best mom. We have to be the best wife. We have to have a clean house, a hot body, and money in the bank. We have to be the boss lady. We have to have the best girlfriends. We have to be the soccer mom that dresses sharp and has a crockpot full of good food in the minivan. But is this life we've imagined in our heads really possible? It sounds like a lot of work and hassle. Instead of creating an image of perfection, why not create an image of progress. We're all trying to have a nice home, nice children, nice relationships, and a nice body. Sometimes nice is good enough. Sometimes we need to say no to things that don't really matter to us, but matter to the image we have in our heads. We need to shatter those images and take life for what it gives us. We will sometimes deal with bad things. We will sometimes have a messy house. Sometimes our kids will be brats. Sometimes we'll let our health go and our bodies will start to say. It's okay. That's life. We need to focus on what's important to us and let the other stuff go, including our grand vision of our perfect life. Life isn't perfect and we shouldn't kill ourselves striving to live up to that expectation. Say no to what doesn't matter so you can say yes to what does.

What can you say 'no' to today?

October 21st

"Resentment is like drinking poison and then hoping it will kill your enemies."
- Nelson Mandela

Sometimes we can be our own worst enemy. We worry about things that we can't control. We feel alone even when we're surrounded by a crowd. We are jealous or envious of another person for what they have. We conjure up stories and put words in other people's mouths. All of these actions do nothing to the other people, but bring stress to ourselves. If we could bring gratitude into our world, and be grateful for being alive, being healthy, and for being around people that love us, we'd realize that projecting our insecurities onto other people isn't worth the effort. We must realize that we need to start with selfishness first, working on our weaknesses first, before we can become helpful to other people. Control what you can control in your life, and don't worry about anything else. Your economy. Your health. Your wealth. Your emotions. Your mentality is all that should matter. Once you've got that handled, then you can contribute and improve others in your environment and community.

What worthless feelings do you need to get rid of today?

October 22nd

"Never doubt that a small group of thoughtful, committed, citizens can change the world. Indeed, it is the only thing that ever has."
-Margaret Mead

Do you belong to a group that's involved with your community? Do you help with your church activities? Do you give money to charitable organizations? People helping people, that's what we're meant to do in life. We all have unique talents and skills and we have a responsibility to share them with the world. Some of it you will be compensated for with money and some of it you will get a return in different ways. Helping others helps yourself. It gives you satisfaction that you're needed. It can boost your endorphins and make you feel good. It can bring meaning and hope to those that are going through a rough time in their lives. One person can always make a difference to someone else. A group of people can impact even more lives. Never think that a small donation or a small act of effort doesn't make a difference because it can. Even if it only helps one person, that person can then help someone else, and the ripple effect takes over. Being thoughtful and committed can certainly bring about change that can help everyone live better lives.

What can you give today?

October 23rd

"The minute you choose to do what you really want to do, it's a different kind of life."
-Buckminster Fuller

I'll go back to school, after the kids are out of the house. I'll lose the weight, after the weather breaks. I'll go for the promotion after Bob moves to another department. We tend to put off the things we really want to do until our circumstances are completely aligned. But in reality, that never happens. In reality, we're afraid of failing at the thing we want to achieve. In reality, we're afraid of the ridicule and opinions from people that we love. We're afraid of the change that needs to happen deep down in order to make things happen. Excuses and procrastination block our dreams from manifesting. In order to change things, we need to change ourselves first. The thoughts and actions that have gotten us to this point in our lives are not the same thoughts and actions needed to get to where we want to go. Something needs to change and it needs to change right now. We can't waste time putting things off. It's our responsibility to live up to our potential and we must start doing that now!

What do you *really* want to do?

October 24th

"Change might not be fast and it isn't always easy. But with time and effort, almost any habit can be reshaped."
-Charles Duhigg, *The Power of Habit: Why We Do What We Do in Life and Business*

No one likes to change. Change is hard. Change takes a lot of energy. Change can sometimes take time to accomplish. But change is necessary in order to grow and improve our lives. How can we get healthier if we don't change the shape and tone of our bodies? How can we build wealth if we don't change the way we spend and invest our money? How can we raise successful children if we lack the character for them to emulate? It's just like driving a car. When we are first learning, we're nervous, we're hitting the brakes hard every minute, and we don't know what we're doing. But two months later, we're more comfortable behind the wheel. And ten years later, we don't even think about it anymore, it comes naturally to us because we've done it a million times before. That's what habits and daily routines are. They are difficult to do at first, and then over time, they become natural and quite easy.

What change do you need to start making today?

October 25th

"There is a thin line that separates laughter and pain, comedy and tragedy, humor and hurt."
- Erma Bombeck

We walk along that small line every day as women. One thing could set us off in one way or the other. Sometimes we allow our emotions to control us. Sometimes we allow our stress and anxiety to consume our thoughts. Sometimes we think that something is a tragedy when in reality, it's a blessing. All of these emotions boil down to our perspective on how we see them. One situation may spark a positive emotion while another situation may spark a negative one. But for another person, the same situations may spark different emotions. If you tend to see things positively, you'll spin your emotions about being hopeful that things will work out. If you tend to see things negatively, you'll spin your emotions about being a victim with no control over the situation. Why walk the line of positive and negative when you can live on just one side? Being positive means that you control the situation. Being positive means that you don't dwell on pain and failure, but for learning from the situation so you can make it better the next time. Reframe the situation and your perspective on the outcome will change and so will your results.

What side of the line do you walk on?

October 26th

"Knowing others is intelligence; knowing yourself is true wisdom. Mastering others is strength; mastering yourself is true power."
– Lao Tzu, Tao Te Ching

What are your habits? What ideas and thoughts do you tend to lean on? What opinions do you have on certain subjects? Do you show up on time, or are you always late? Do you procrastinate on finishing things, or do you work until you get the project done? Are you hopeful and optimistic, or dreadful and pessimistic? Are you responsible for the things that happen to you, or do you blame others for your misfortune and play the victim of circumstance? Knowing what your true tendencies are can help you work on improving them, or avoiding them altogether. If you know that you're always late, you can mark the event in your calendar at an earlier time so that you can arrive on time. If you know you procrastinate, you can schedule time every day to work on the project until it's finished. If you're pessimistic, you can find all of the things that *can* go wrong with a task and get your negativity out of the way so you can focus on what *could* go right with the task and then just do it without hesitation. If you're aware of your downfalls, you can do things that will neutralize them, giving you the results you really want.

How can you work around your faults today?

October 27th

"Hide not your talents, they for use were made. What's a sundial in the shade?"
- Benjamin Franklin

Are you living up to your potential? Do you hit your targets and goals on a continuous basis? Do you surround yourself with supportive people? Are you constantly learning new things? Are you continuously improving your mindset, your character, and your life? Are you sharing your skills with the world? As women, we often think that our talents aren't worthy of sharing. They don't matter. They won't make a difference. Sometimes we think we're supposed to act in a certain way because of an expectation from someone close to us. This is nonsense and doesn't serve anyone. As free women, we have the right and duty to be the best people we can be. We have the right and duty to change our family trees. We have the right and duty to be happy, healthy, and wealthy. If we don't have the skills needed to live the life we want, we have the freedom to learn those skills and implement them in our own lives. Do you know what you want? Do you know who you want to become? It's never too late to improve your life and live up to your potential.

What are your talents?

October 28th

"I can calculate the motion of heavenly bodies but not the madness of people."
-Isaac Newton

Some women are unpredictable. Others are more cautious and precise. Some women take control of their situations while others create drama. Some women focus their attention on the people they love, while others focus on their shallow pursuits. Whichever side of the coin you're on, decide today that you won't get caught up in other people's problems. Life can be easy and full of happiness and joy if you concentrate on being level-headed. Crazy women attract crazy situations in their lives. It's almost like they invite chaos open handedly. If you think you're one of those women who thrives on chaos and uncertainty, you'll never truly be happy because you'll always be looking for more chaos and uncertainty. Your life will always be out of control and you'll always be frantic and unscrupulous. Learn to control your emotions and your actions to allow logic to prevail. This will attract success and happiness into your life.

What madness is in your life?

October 29th

"Yesterday I was clever, so I wanted to change the world. Today I am wise, so I am changing myself."
- Mawlana Jalal-al-Din Rumi

We can't help others until we help ourselves. We must read history and philosophy as it pertains to our own lives and communities. We must learn new skills. We must improve our patience for others. We must have a hopeful and positive outlook on life. We must take control of our emotions and our actions. We must get rid of the distractions that steal our time and energy. We must control what we can, and leave the rest alone. We must become better listeners. We must become better friends. We must become better lovers. We must become better mothers. When we improve ourselves, the rest of our environment improves because we have an improved outlook on life and we can help in a more beneficial way. Our world starts within us, and we must become better women so that our children can build strong characters.

What things do you want to change about yourself?

October 30th

"The ultimate measure of a person is not her mistakes or accomplishments, but what she does with them."
-Liza Wiemer

Are you living your dream life? Are you building wealth? Are you watching your diet and exercising on a regular basis? Are you positive? Are you helpful? Do you have a loving relationship? Are you successful? Do you have some fun girlfriends? If not, why? Are you allowing your anxiety and fear to control your actions? Are you afraid to get out of your comfort zone and try something new? Have you been dumped before and don't want to get back in the dating pool? Do you think that other people deserve a good life and not you? Are you stuck? Are you overweight? Are you frustrated with your life? We all go through times of success and failure, what matters is how you build on them? If you're playing the victim role, you'll never take the responsibility for your own actions nor your own success, and you'll leave it in the hands of someone else. If you allow yourself to be controlled by other people or circumstances, you won't experience the freedom of living your life on your terms and will become enslaved by it. Is this really how you want to live?

How do you deal with achievements and failures?

October 31st

"Children pay little attention to their parents' teachings, but reproduce their characters faithfully."
-Mason Cooley

Children don't necessarily listen to the words that we say to them but they do mimic our habits. They see how we interact with our environment. They see how we deal with people. They experience what kind of mood we're in on a daily basis. They see our outlook on life. They see us for who we really are and they implement these characteristics into their own lives. Good or bad, our children soak in their environment. If we want our children to grow up healthy, wealthy, and wise, we must demonstrate those qualities in our daily routines. We must show them what it's like to be healthy. We must show them what it's like to be wealthy. We must show them what it's like to be wise. If we don't demonstrate those things, how will our children do it? You can't teach what you don't know. You can't teach a way of living that you're not experiencing yourself. It's impossible. So make sure your children see the strong, vibrant, and positive woman that you are so they can learn to be the same when they're adults.

What are you teaching your children?

November

Hey Lady,

The year is winding down. Now is a great time to look over your goals you've been working towards all year. Are you progressing? Are you getting closer to achieving any of them? Or did you forget about them and you're stuck in the same place as last year.

No worries, girl! I've got your back. Grab a sheet of paper and think about all the things you want to do. Get in shape. Find a lover. Move to another city. Buy that new car. Pay off your student loans. Whatever goals you have, write it down. Skip a few spaces in between. Okay, now think about what the first three steps are that will help you achieve that goal. Just the first three steps. Once you've figured out what they are, then write down when you can start. If you said tomorrow, you're wrong. Today is the perfect day to take the first step on all of them. No matter how small or simple the first step is, you'll find relief in the fact that you started. Take a walk around the block with the dog. Go to a party with a new outfit on. Send out your resume. Save your first $50. Create a budget.

November 1st

"It is the mark of an educated mind to be able to entertain a thought without accepting it."

-Aristotle, *Metaphysics*

Women in general like to gossip or listen to gossip. Some women take gossip as fact while others tend to believe that there's a little truth in all of it. True intelligence gathers facts before creating an opinion or judgment. Another thing to think about is how influential are you? Are you easily influenced by those around you? Jim Rohn said that you are the sum of the five people you're around the most. Who is in your inner circle and are they the best people to be around? Are they negative? Are they always talking smack about others? Are they good mothers? If you're easily influenced, you may become like those other people. But is this really you? Is this how you want to live your life? Creating opinions and judgments about something without educating yourself on it, can lead to prejudice, hypocrisy, and hatred for no reason. Do yourself a favor and stay away from negative people.

Who is in your immediate circle that is negative and detrimental to your life? Can you ignore them? Can you get rid of them?

November 2nd

"To lose confidence in one's body is to lose confidence in oneself."
-Simone de Beauvoir

100% of women have wrinkles. 90% have cellulite. All of our boobs will hang to the floor. Yet, women are viewed as creatures of beauty. Men crave us. They fight for our love. They act like buffoons in order to get our attention. When will we stop criticizing ourselves and start loving ourselves for what we are? We all have flaws. We all have scars. If someone loves us, it doesn't matter to them. So what should it matter to us? We all have something about ourselves that we don't like. We want straight hair when it's curly. We want to be tall when we are short. We want to be thin when we are fat. Wishing we were something other than ourselves gets us nowhere fast. Be confident in your body and others will notice and be drawn to you.

What do I love about my body? What do I hate that I can change?

November 3rd

"Modesty brings nothing except good."
-Prophet Muhammad

You don't have to dress sexy to be sexy. You don't have to sleep with countless people to feel worthy. It all starts from within. What you think about yourself is what others will think of you. If you're confident, it doesn't matter how you dress or what car you drive. You can be wealthy and confident without flaunting it. There's a lot to be said for humility and grace. Men are visual creatures and will treat you as such if you show too much skin. They won't take you seriously and they will lust after your physicality. Why give them the satisfaction? Dress professionally and conduct yourself with elegance and strength and you will be seen as such. If you want that kind of attention, it's easy to get, but you may not like the consequences. Don't play with fire unless you are prepared to get burned.

What can you do today to portray modesty and humbleness?

November 4th

"Everything in life is figureoutable."
-Marie Forleo, *Everything is Figureoutable*

We may need help. We may stumble. We may fail. That's okay, but if we persist and don't give up, we'll figure it out. If it's been done before, we can also do it. If the diet works for her, it will work for us. If we follow the instructions, the crib will be put together correctly. If we follow our mentor's instructions, we can get the same results as she did. Our lives are not different from any other women's throughout history. We love. We lose. We win. It's all the same thing. What are you going to do to get the things you want in life? What woman must you become in order to succeed? It's not about perfection, it's about progress.

What steps do you need to figure out to improve your life?

November 5th

"You are not stuck where you are unless you decide to be."
- Wayne W. Dyer

Our life is made up of results that come from actions we take on a continuous basis. We believe in a certain world perspective and we act accordingly. What if our perspective is wrong? What if our beliefs are wrong? What if we can live the life we desire and deserve? What if our present circumstances don't necessarily equal our future experience? What if we can change anything and everything about our life? What if we can succeed? What if we can find the love of our life? What if we can have the family we've always wanted? What if we can make a difference in the world? What if? The possibilities are endless. We only remain in the same place in our lives if we chose to stay there. If we're content in our lives, then why would we change them. But most women are not content. They want more and better. If that is the case, then different actions will need to be taken in order to enjoy different results. Being stuck in one place won't get you to your next destination. You've got to start moving if you're going to end up in another spot. Learn how to get there and start walking.

What steps do you need to take today to stop being stuck?

November 6th

"We have the power to hold no opinion about a thing and to not let it upset our state of mind- for things have no natural power to shape our judgements."
-Marcus Aurelius, *Meditations 6.52.*

Women are opinionated. We tend to tell everyone, even people we don't know, about our opinions. We like to gossip. We like to talk. But sometimes our opinions can get us in trouble. Sometimes our opinions can cause conflict where it's not intended. It's okay to not have an opinion about something. Or if you do have an opinion that doesn't match another person, to keep it to yourself. Do you really want to waste your time arguing with someone you don't care about over something that's not really important? Do you have to be right all the time? Why do you think your opinion is superior to mine? In reality, you're no more important than anyone else, so why must you spout off your mouth when given the chance. In reality, silence is golden. Sometimes people talk just to talk without giving any value in the conversation. Is this you? If so, take a step back and reflect on what's being said before you give your empty suggestion. Most people only care about themselves, so why waste your energy trying to convince them otherwise?

Today's challenge: Can you hold your opinion to yourself today when confronted by someone?

November 7th

"Let all your efforts be directed to something, let it keep that end in view. It's not activity that disturbs people, but false conceptions of things that drive them mad."

–Seneca, *On Tranquility of Mind, 12.5.*

Living with intention. Being focused on living the life you want. Enjoying friends and family. Keeping your mind and body healthy. Avoiding conflict. Being useful. Helping others. Not allowing outside influences to derail your efforts. If we can keep our attention and focus on the things that matter to us and get rid of the things that don't, we'd be in a much better place. We could live without stress and anxiety. Without constant pressure to be someone we're not. To use our resources in order to make our lives worthwhile and find happiness. Sounds great, right?

What are you doing today to live intentionally?

November 8th

"Being both soft and strong is a combination very few have mastered."
-Yasmin Mogahed

Why are strong women called bitches? Why are they ruthless, cold, and relentless? Why are men considered driven, ambitious, and focused? Why the double standard? Can a woman be strong and soft at the same time? We're supposed to conquer the world, but be a perfect mother and wife when we get home. Where's the energy in that? The definition of men and women have been blurred over the past century. We need to redefine what being a woman means. We can be strong, soft and curvy, and creative. We can be anything we want because we live in a free nation. We need to support other women and help us all rise to be the best people we can be.

What are you doing to be the best woman you can be?

November 9th

"Life is really simple, but we insist on making it complicated."
-Confucius

What is our life supposed to be? Are we supposed to struggle and be stressed all the time? Are we supposed to be broke and miserable? Are we supposed to be overweight and out of breath? These are the different ways that most Americans live their lives in the 21st century. We can't rub two nickels together because we spend all of our money on our wants and not our needs. We are lazy and rely on restaurants and fast food joints to give us nutrition. We take jobs we hate and surround ourselves with negative people. Life shouldn't be this way. We should be happy. We should be healthy and wealthy. We should have family and friends around us who support us and love us. We should have a successful career that fulfills us and allows us to contribute to society. That's a good life. It's simple and we should embrace the simplicity of it all and see where it takes us throughout our life journey.

What can you do today to simplify your life?

November 10th

"Every action has its pleasures and its price."
-Socrates

This is called the opportunity cost. If you work late at the office, you miss dinner and family time with your kids. If you spend your extra money on a pair of boots that are similar to ones you already have, you miss out on going out with your friends. If you lay around and watch a movie, you miss out on having a good workout that can keep you trim. Every action we take has its costs, both good and bad. If we spend our money one way, we can't spend it in another way. If we waste our time and energy doing something mundane, we don't have it when we want to do something useful or fun. We need to be more aware of the opportunity costs when it relates to our finite resources. Our time, money, and energy. We need to focus our efforts on using them to our advantage and not to others. To spend them being around the people we love. To spend them doing what we love to do. To spend them on what matters to us. Then we can pay any price that we're asked to pay.

How can you spend your resources wisely today?

November 11th

"The beginning is the most important part of the work."

Plato, *The Republic*

Getting out of debt. Starting a new workout schedule. Trying a new job. Going on the first date. Giving birth to your first child. Applying for college. There's hundreds of first times we all face during our lives. The hardest step we take is always the first one. It's the first step that we wander out of our comfort zones and can be scary. But this first step is the most important step that we can take in order to improve our lives and grow. Once we take that first step, we can realize that the big bad world we were scared of, isn't that scary. Then we take the next step, and then the next, and then the next until finally we arrive at our goal. But it all starts with that first step.

What first step are you going to take today?

November 12th

"Life begins at the end of your comfort zone."
-Neale Donald Walsh

We love our comfort zones. We love security. We love to feel safe. But what kind of fun is that? What kind of adventures can we have when we stay home, sitting on our couch in our sweatpants, eating a bag of chips, and watching Netflix? Is it fun to watch stories of other people's lives? Sometimes it is. But why not make your life into an interesting story? Why not take a chance on something that you've wanted to do for a long time but haven't gotten the nerve to? Why not ask that guy or gal out? Why not move to that new city and take that new job that could be the opportunity of a lifetime? Why not start paying down your debt and live debt-free? Staying safe and locked in your comfort zone makes you bored. It can make you sad and depressed. It can keep you from becoming the person that you're meant to be, living the life you're meant to live. Do everyone a favor and get out of your comfort zone today!

What can you do that's new today?

November 13th

"I know I have but the body of a weak and feeble woman, but I have the heart and stomach of a king, and of a king of England too."
-Queen Elizabeth I

Women are seen as the weaker sex. What we lack in physical strength, we make up for in mental and spiritual strength. We love deeper. We can persevere through any situation. We can tear down a city with a change of opinion. We cause wars for our love. We have the freedom to be, do, and have anything we want in this country. We can make plans and we can break them. We can directly influence policy reform. We are beautiful inside and out. We need to remember this. We may not be physically as strong as men, but we are superior in too many ways to count. Act like the queen you truly are today. Be strong but gracious. Be tactful but determined. Follow your heart and keep your head level. If you can do this, anyone, even a man will respect you and listen to you.

How can you be strong today?

November 14th

"Being brave means that knowing when you fail, you won't fail forever."
– Lana Del Rey

Failure is but a step along the path to our goals. It does not define us. It does not consume us. It does not defeat us. We can only fail at something if we quit. Sometimes we do need to quit in order to get us on a different path. Sometimes we need to pivot. But that doesn't mean that failure is our identity. It only means that we needed to take a different direction along the way. Deciding when to pivot is important along with ways to grow and improve. Progress sometimes consists of two steps forward and one step back. Or another step sideways. It's the woman that keeps moving forward no matter what happens, who perseveres and lives the life she desires and deserves.

What have you failed at in the past?

November 15th

"A book holds a house of gold."
-Chinese Proverb

The golden wisdom that can be learned by reading can make anyone happy, healthy, and rich. Reading about the struggles and victories of previous generations is priceless information. Yet, we tend to forget about history and the wisdom that people have figured out that have lived before us. It's a shame. There's so much wisdom from the past that has been forgotten and ignored. We must wake up and use that knowledge and experience to build a better tomorrow. We can be selfish and use that knowledge to make our own lives better. Start to read about subjects that can make different areas of your life better. Finances. Health and nutrition. Relationships. Sales. Mindset. Investing. DIY. Reading about different ideas and actions can help you implement those improvements in your own life. This can help you make a quantum leap in any area. Use your local library for free resources like books, audiobooks, and magazines. Use YouTube to watch videos on how to fix things or exercise. When you open your mind to new ideas, your beliefs and limitations can be altered and your life forever changed.

What book are you going to start today?

November 16th

"You can say 'no' with respect, you can say 'no' promptly, and you can say 'no' with a lead to someone who might say yes."
-Seth Godin

Why do we feel guilty saying 'no'? Why do we feel like we must be everything to everyone? Why do we give priority to everyone else rather than to what *we* want? It started during the women's movement. We went from being housewives and stay-at-home moms to bosses, employees, housewives, and moms. So we doubled our jobs. So now we get to work all day and handle the stresses from our boss and customers to coming home and doing the chores, being a wife, and being a mom. Wow, that sounds like a fun job to sign up for! An easy mindset that can remove all of the stresses from your complicated life is the simple word 'no.' Not obligating yourself to activities that you don't want to do helps to free you from them. Not worrying about getting the house clean today helps to release the anxiety that you have. Not comparing yourself to the other soccer mom who looks like she has it all together only to find out that deep inside she feels helpless and exhausted can make you feel relieved. No one puts expectations on you except yourself. When you accept the challenge, then you must live up to it. An easy way to take care of the problem is to not accept the challenge in the first place. Instead, focus on one thing at a time that can make you happy and the people that really matter to you.

What obligations can you get rid of today?

November 17th

"Don't interpret anything too much. This is time waster number one."
- Dee Dee Artner

We worry that something *might* happen. We pace back and forth hoping things will work out for the better. We pray that our loved ones are safe. We spend a lot of time and energy trying to control outcomes that we have no control over and it's a complete waste of our resources. Instead of wasting time worrying and hoping for something, the only thing we can do is to put ourselves in the best position for success as we can and allow fate to intervene. We need to move on with our lives and stop wasting it on dissecting every little detail. We need to stop wasting time on putting words in other people's mouths and trying to figure out what they *actually* mean. When dealing with men, it's very simple. If they say something, that's what they mean. They've very simple creatures. If they don't call, they don't want to talk to you. If they say no, they mean not right now. If you're dealing with women who can be more complicated, you can simply ask for clarification on the matter at hand and then you know exactly what's going on and you can get on with your day. Stop wasting time interpreting things that don't need interpreting.

Are you wasting time trying to interpret something?

November 18th

"Your world is only as small as you make it."
- Gabrielle Union , *We're Going to Need More Wine*

Your life has endless possibilities. You can live anywhere you want. You can be anything you want. You can surround yourself with anyone you want to spend time with. If you want to be a bum, you can be a bum. If you want to live in the same town as you grew up in, the choice is yours. But if you want to break out of your comfort zone, you certainly can do that. You can travel. You can learn new skills that can earn you a promotion in another city. You can create wealth. You can lead an active and healthy lifestyle. The world is a vast place and you can take advantage of as much or as little of it as you want. If you want to accomplish big things, you can. If you want to lead a more simple life, you can. It's up to you, your imagination, your skills, your imagination, and your courage. Take some time today and think how big you want your life to be.

How big do you want your life to be?

November 19th

"Life is too short for negativity. Focus all your energy to create happiness."
- Banani Ray

The news media says we're headed for a recession and a stock market crash. The Democrats did this. The Republicans did that. Your neighbor is complaining that your dog is barking too much or your cat is tearing up his plants. Your boss is grumpy and yelling at everyone. They got your order wrong at the drive thru and now you have to go inside to correct it. Every day we have challenges and negative occurrences. That doesn't mean that we can contribute to it. That doesn't mean we have to let it ruin our day. We can take the bumps and obstacles that come our way and do the best we can to get around them. Tomorrow's a new day and we don't have to take home the crap we go through during the day. We can take a deep breath and know that we can get through anything. Maybe our boss is having trouble at home. Can we give him some grace? Maybe we need to stop listening to the news media and focus on our own lives and what we can control. Maybe your neighbor lost his dog and is jealous that you have one. You never know what other people are going through. Give grace and focus your energy on having a happy life.

How can you ignore the negativity today?

November 20th

"The grass is greener on the other side, but often this is just an illusion. Most probably, everyone is as unhappy as you."
- Marcella Purnama, *What I Wish I Had Known*

Have you ever looked at another woman and thought she's so lucky? Maybe she married a rich man. Maybe she's beautiful. Maybe her kids are star athletes. But maybe she's not happy. Maybe her husband works all of the time and ignores her. Maybe she knows she's beautiful but there's nothing deeper to her personality and she knows that her beauty is fading. Maybe her kids are spoiled brats and are arrogant and very mean to other kids. We never really know what's going on behind closed doors. We don't really know what other people are feeling or going through. We're all human and we all have the same issues. Even if our outside world looks perfect. So don't compare your own life with someone else's. You're doing great and you should be grateful for all the love and success you are already experiencing!

Is the grass greener on the other side?

November 21st

"Time is the single most important resource that we have. Every single minute we lose is never coming back."
-Tarun Sharma

What price do you put on your time? Most of us give our time to others for free and don't personally benefit from it. We constantly spend our time making cupcakes for our kids' class party, doing chores, running around to activities, helping a coworker with their project, or doing a DIY project to save money. But what is your time really worth? Is it worth doing all of these things for free? Wealthy people buy their time because they know how valuable it is. They hire other people to do things for them whether it's sales calls or grabbing their dry cleaning and mowing their lawn. Not everyone is wealthy, but is there any way you can buy some time so that you have more of it to spend on things that really matter to you?

How can you buy some time today?

November 22nd

"The first source of advice you should listen to is your instinct. "
- Mitta Xinindlu

Most women have a very intuitive 6th sense. We can feel the mood in the room. We can feel if something isn't right. We can feel if there's something troubling to the person we're talking to. Our intuition helps guide us in the right direction and protect us from harm. Whether we listen to our intuition is another subject. Most men are action takers.They want to solve all the problems with their brute force. Women on the other hand, want to think about things and make sure that it's the right action to take. That's where our instincts come into play. There's nothing wrong with taking our time and thinking about a decision before we act on it. That's a good way to avoid making a major mistake. There's another opinion that says we should go for it no matter what and not listen to ration but rather than our desires. However you live your life is up to you, but if you're in tune with your instincts and intuition, no action or decision you make will be the wrong one.

What are your instincts telling you to do today?

November 23rd

Happiness will never come to those who fail to appreciate what they already have.
-Buddha

It's Thanksgiving week. If we're lucky, we'll be gathering with family and celebrate our lives with food and conversation. Preparing the feast is always hard work, but realize that the feast represents the love and bounty that you are lucky to have. Thanksgiving is a time to be thankful and grateful for all that you have. You've survived. You're alive. You have a beautiful life surrounded by the people you love. It's a time to reflect on what's right and to start making plans on correcting what's wrong. Take a moment during this chaotic week and feel the abundance and happiness that The Universe and God has surrounded you with. As Martha Stewart says, "It's a good thing!"

What are you grateful for today?

November 24th

"Maybe that's worse, not letting ourselves be loved. Because we're too afraid of giving ourselves to someone we might lose."
–Mitch Albom, *Tuesdays with Morrie*

We get dumped. We get shunned. We get ridiculed. We get criticized. We love and we lose. We start and we finish. It's the Law of rhythm- everything works in a cycle. Just because we've experienced negativity, doesn't mean that we shouldn't brush ourselves off and get back in the game. We are meant to love. We help one another. We listen and offer sympathy, empathy, and a shoulder to cry on. If someone doesn't want to be in your life anymore, that's their loss! There's another person who's looking for someone as wonderful as you are and is longing to meet you. Don't close off the opportunity to live a happy life because some bozo decided to move in a different direction. Everyone experiences loss and rejection. All of it gives you life experience and something to talk about with your girlfriends. Dust yourself off and start fresh. That's what strong women do.

What are you afraid of?

November 25th

"A day of Rest is always needed."
-Solange Nicole

We work hard. We run around constantly with the kids and their activities. We cook, we clean, and we try to spend time with our spouses and friends. We run, run, run, and then we get sick. What that's telling us is that we run ourselves in the ground and there's no reason for it. We need to stop and take some time for ourselves. We need to relax and rest. Today is a great day to visit the spa. Get a massage or a manicure. Draw a bubble bath, lock the door, and let the warm water melt away our stress. Take a nap. Tell everyone no. Today is your day. With the busy holiday season amongst us, today is a great day to wind down, grab a coffee or tea, a warm blanket, and veg out with a good book all afternoon. Take the day off work and enjoy the quiet house. You deserve this time to yourself. Spend it wisely.

How can you rest and relax today?

November 26th

"Sometimes the worst-tasting crap is the best for you."
-Michael Harmon, *Brutal*

We've just enjoyed Thanksgiving and all of the yummy carbs that go along with that meal. The mashed potatoes. The stuffing. The homemade pumpkin pie. It's non-stop gluttony all day causing you to need a nap. You may wake up today and your pants are a little snugger or you're feeling tired even though you just had a good night's sleep. That's the carb overload. Your body is tired from processing all of the excess foods. Today is a good day for a reset. Let's get some green stuff in your system. Of course it doesn't taste as good as the yummy homemade food you just indulged in, but your body needs it. Grab some veggies and have a big ol' salad for lunch today or get out the blender and make a green smoothie. This will help keep your immune system strong during the cold winter months. As the holidays and the parties creep up, don't forget to add some fresh veggies in your diet. It will keep you from getting sick and missing out on all the fun.

Did you eat anything green today?

November 27th

"Let us be grateful to the people who make us happy; they are the charming gardeners who make our souls blossom."
-Marcel Proust

We just enjoyed Thanksgiving and spent some time with our families. Now we're headed into the holiday season. Even if you don't have any relatives close to you, you still have friends that love you. Today is a great day to feel grateful for your life and everyone in it. Fill today with your favorite things. Call your bestie and have lunch with her. Make your favorite meal. Listen to your favorite artist or watch your favorite movie. Feel the happiness and gratefulness of being alive and being surrounded with your favorite things and your favorite people.

What makes you happy?

November 28th

"If you think you must wait for an apology to forgive, you may not have that chance. Just forgive and find the peace you need."
-Gift Gugu Mona, *The True Value of Forgiveness: Quotes and Sayings*

Sometimes we fight with people. Sometimes we're disappointed. Should we waste our lives in pain and suffering because of it? Or should we forgive and move on? Everyone is human. We all make mistakes. Forgiving someone for their mistakes means that you have freed yourself to continue with your own life without depending on them nor their actions. Forgiving someone takes guts. It doesn't mean you're a doormat. It doesn't mean that you forget that they hurt you. And it doesn't mean that your relationship will ever be the same as it was in the past. But what it does is allow you to concentrate on what you can control, and that's yourself and your own thoughts, feelings, and actions. If you can remain in control of yourself, then no one can ever harm you again because you simply move on with your own life, not depending on them acting in a certain way. You're free. Use that freedom to your advantage.

Who do you need to forgive?

November 29th

"Just like the sun dispels the shadows of the night each morning, embracing your heart's true desire is the only way to dispel fear and doubt."
- Imania Margria, *Eyes*

When we imagine what we want and then take the steps necessary to get it, we gain wisdom and discipline along the way. We also gain crucial experience that can help us in future endeavors. Everyone has doubts and fears along the way, but successful women know that those doubts and fears have no merit and are only there to hold us back from getting what we want. All of the courage and energy that's needed to be successful is already in us. All we have to do is tap into our inner Goddess, our inner Warrior and find the strength and determination to pursue our dreams. If you want it, go get it. It's not difficult to be successful, but you must believe in yourself first and not allow others to distract you or put false narratives in your mind. You live in one of the best countries in the world, it's your duty and responsibility to fulfill your destiny. You must take advantage of all the luxuries that life has to offer you. When you do this, all of your doubt and silly fear will melt away.

What do you really want?

November 30th

"Disconnecting from some people is as important as connecting with some people."
- Garima Soni

Over the years, we tend to accumulate a lot of things, including people and relationships. Some of these relationships turn out to be important to our lives while others are not. Some people are supportive and are true friends when you need help while others are not. Some people want to see you succeed and don't have an agenda with you, while others only take and don't contribute. You must ask yourself if it's time to declutter your life. Is it time to get rid of the people that aren't making a positive change in your life? Is it time to end friendships that aren't serving you? Sometimes this means that people that you've known your whole life will need to be forgotten. Sometimes this means that family members will have to go. It's okay. As we grow, so does the group of people we grow with. That's part of life. Don't be afraid of distancing yourself from anyone that doesn't hold your friendship as an important connection in their life.

Who do you need to let go of?

December

Hey Lady,

Wow! It's the end of the year already. Now is the time to enjoy with your family and friends. You've already started working on your goals for next year, so you won't have to waste any time planning anything. They are already underway and now you can have fun with the holiday parties and festivities.

Make sure that you remember what this time is for. You may be religious and celebrate Hanukkah or Christmas. You may love to ski and want to hit the slopes at the lodge. You may find yourself at the gym enjoying your child's sport's team. Whatever occasion you find yourself in, reflect on your life over the past year and find gratitude in all the bounty that God and the Universe has blessed you with. Be grateful for your health, that you have a warm house to sleep in at night, in the love you're surrounded by, and for the opportunities you have to live in the greatest nation on Earth. Not every woman has the freedom that you have. Be grateful that you were born at this time and in this great place.

If you find that your life needs to improve, take the time to figure out what that looks like and start moving towards it. Imagine what your life could look like if things were going your way. Then start taking the actions necessary in order to make them happen. You've got this girl! I believe in you! You're beautiful and strong and can do anything you want to do!

Happy Holidays!

December 1st

"Courage is knowing what not to fear."
- Plato

We can get things in our head that aren't real. We worry about things that haven't happened yet. We play out different scenarios that may or may not occur. We save for a rainy day. We do things, just in case. All of this anxiety and stress comes from fear. Fear in the unknown. Fear of what can go wrong. Fear of the future. Fear. An antidote to fear is knowledge. Belief. Certainty. If you can decipher between fact and fiction, wouldn't it be easier to feel more confident? If you could learn how to get around an obstacle through knowledge and practice, wouldn't your path seem more clear? Having courage is The Universe's way of leading you to water. To drink so you don't die of thirst. Courage is the nudge you need to get out of your comfort zone and to follow your dreams. It's courage that gets rid of fear. It's courage that helps you change your beliefs and create certainty in your life. Fear has no room in successful women. It's fear that will hold you back and it will be fear that gives you the same results year after year. Get out of your own way and let the lioness come out of her cage!

What do you fear?

December 2nd

"When you are content to be simply yourself and don't compare or compete, everyone will respect you."
– Lao Tzu, *Tao Te Ching*

Comparison can be lethal. It can create depression. It can create a lack. It can create anxiety. Why do we want her butt? Why do we want her spouse? Why do we want her life? She's no better than you are. She's no more beautiful than you. Or smarter. Or luckier. But one thing she is, she's courageous and she's content in her own skin. She's comfortable being herself. She makes no excuses. She gets what she wants and she doesn't apologize for it. That makes her beautiful. That makes her sexy. That gets her a wonderful spouse. That gives her a wonderful life. You can do the same thing, but you have to be confident in your own skin and develop the talents you were given. It starts from within.

Who do you compare yourself to? What makes you unique?

December 3rd

"When it hurts, observe. Life is trying to teach you something.
-Buddha

Our bodies are made to experience pain. Pain helps to protect us. Pain alerts us to run and be safe. What about our emotions? Women cry. That's what we do when we're frustrated, sad, or even overwhelmingly happy. It's a signal to our brains that something is wrong or extreme. Be aware of your emotions. Be aware of your body. How do you feel? If something isn't right, go get it checked. See a doctor. See a counselor. In order to live the life you deserve, you need your mind and your body to be working on all cylinders. If something isn't right, fix it.

What area of your life is hurting you?

December 4th

"Change your life today. Don't gamble on the future, act now, without delay."

–Simone de Beauvoir, *The Book of Positive Quotations*

We only live once as far as we know. If we live to be 80, that's around 4000 weeks. Seems small, doesn't it? If you're unhappy with something in your life, why live that way? Why don't you change it? Why suffer when you can thrive? Why be frustrated? Life's too short. You can accomplish anything you want. It won't be easy. It will take time and lots of energy but anything is possible. Don't waste the precious time you've been given. Go get what you want, not just for you, but for your family and your community. They all need you to succeed.

What do you want to change in your life? What step can you take today to start the change?

December 5th

"Once you make a decision, the universe conspires to make it happen."
-Ralph Waldo Emerson

Making a decision is the first step in moving towards a new goal. If you decide to increase your income or lose 20 pounds, your subconscious mind starts looking for ways in order to create that reality. Are there people out there earning the money you want to earn? Yes. Okay, then it's possible. What do you have to do in order to start earning that kind of money? Those are the questions your mind starts asking itself. What about losing 20 pounds? Are there people out there living at a lighter weight? Yes. Okay, then it's possible. What do you have to do in order to start living at that weight? Those are the questions your mind starts asking itself. Once it asks those questions, it's now on the lookout for the answers. Those answers are the action plans you'll need to take in order to accomplish the goals you're after. You don't have to know how you're going to accomplish it at first. The plan will be discovered after you make the decision to pursue it. Then opportunities to realize your goal will be identified in front of you. It all starts with a decision.

What decision can you make today to start a new goal?

December 6th

"*Wealth* is measured in time, while *rich* is measured in money."
-Robert Kiyosaki, *Rich Dad Poor Dad*

76% of Americans live paycheck to paycheck. If you didn't have a paycheck, how long would you survive? A week? A month? A few years? It is important to get our financial life right in order to build wealth. We must live debt-free. We must save money, gold, and silver in case we need to tap into our reserves for an emergency. We must diversify our investments into stock dividends, real estate, commodities, and business ownership. If your investments pay you monthly, you're creating wealth. We must get rid of the jealousy and envy we have of others that have the material things that we think make them rich. They may look rich on the outside, bút be living like a pauper on the inside. You can either look rich, or you can be wealthy.

What are you doing today to build long-term wealth?

December 7th

"One, remember to look up at the stars and not down at your feet. Two, never give up work. Work gives you meaning and purpose and life is empty without it. Three, if you are lucky enough to find love, remember it is there and don't throw it away."
– Stephen Hawking

A happy life. That's what we all strive to have. But we can't allow it to happen or allow others to influence it negatively. We have to create it by our own thoughts and actions. What do we really want? A great career? Money in the bank? A loving relationship? A family? A tropical vacation? Anything is possible if we do the work. It takes work on ourselves before results can manifest. We need to have a positive attitude. We must be willing to help others solve their problems. We must be courageous and daring. We must be creative. We must be loving. We must be grateful for the progress we've made thus far. Then and only then can we reach for the stars and live a meaningful life.

What is meaningful to me?

December 8th

"Do what you can, with what you have, where you are."
-Theodore Roosevelt

Women tend to think that others are special. *She grew up with money. She was lucky to have met him when she did. Her family helped her. She had kids really late. She was beautiful and doors opened up for her.* Whatever excuse you're telling yourself about the reason why you're not successful is garbage and you know it. Everyone starts from the bottom. Everyone starts from the beginning. You won't know what you're doing at first. You won't have all the resources you need to make your idea happen. But don't allow that to stop you from getting started. Work with the cards you've been dealt and see what kind of game you can play. Excuses will never get you started. Comparison will only keep you in your safety zone.

What can you do today to start hitting your goals?

December 9th

Your beauty should not come from outward adornment, such as elaborate hairstyles and the wearing of gold jewelry or fine clothes. Rather, it should be that of your inner self, the unfading beauty of a gentle and quiet spirit, which is of great worth in God's sight.

-The Holy Bible 1 Peter 3:3-4

We tend to be envious of other women's beauty. Some women have symmetrical eyes and curves that make men swoon. Some women have long dark hair or pouty lips that want to be kissed. Some women are thin and can eat anything they want. But all women are beautiful! It's not what you look like on the outside that makes you beautiful, it's what's on the inside that counts. You will look beautiful if your heart and soul are beautiful. You help others. You give your best every day. You're nurturing and caring. You work hard. You're humble and learn from your mistakes. You're smart and continue improving your skills. Even if you're not considered beautiful on the outside, if you have a strong character, you will radiate beauty with everything you do in life.

What things make you beautiful?

December 10th

"You have everything you need for complete peace and total happiness right now."
– Wayne W. Dyer

Most women love to shop. They want that special facial cream or those pair of boots that they see their favorite influencer wearing. They need to go to the gym so they attract a mate. They think that they must make more money so they can buy anything they want. But material goods will never make you happy. Happiness always comes from within. Satisfaction and contentment come from knowing who you are and when enough is enough. We should all want to improve our lives, but there's a point at which we've reached a level of satisfaction with what we've accomplished. Then it's time to look around and be grateful for what we have and for how far we've come. Then we can feel happiness and complete peace with our lives.

What makes you happy right now?

December 11th

"A woman has to live her life, or live to repent not having lived it."
– D.H. Lawrence, *Lady Chatterley's Lover*

Most people regret something on their deathbed. They regret not spending more time with their loved ones. They regret not taking a chance when they had it. They regret not changing something in their life. They regret not doing more of what they loved. Why spend your days living in regret? Today is the perfect time to make a change. Today is a perfect time to plan a trip somewhere you've always wanted to visit. Today is the perfect day to spend time with someone you love. Today is the perfect day to take that chance. Why wait for tomorrow, or next week when the time is right, or next year when the economy is better? Today is the day! Today is the perfect time to live the life you've always wanted to live! Don't wait! Start living your best life today! With no regrets!

How do you want to start living your best life today?

December 12th

"Humility is royalty without a crown."
-Spencer Kimball

Some of us tend to be arrogant. Gossiping to everyone and anyone that listens to us about our great achievements. Some of us think we're the best thing that's ever happened on this Earth. And in a way, these people are correct. Everyone is unique and special in their own way. But some people hoist themselves on their pedestal and look down on others who are not in the same position. They ridicule them. They scoff at them. They make them feel unworthy. This is no way to build self confidence. Everyone brings something different to the table and should be recognized and appreciated in doing so. Not to be ridiculed or mocked. Being humble and kind creates an unbreakable confidence in anyone displaying both qualities. If you're confident in yourself and your abilities without boasting or taking anything away from anyone else, you are truly a powerful woman and others will recognize your strength.

How can you show humility today?

December 13th

"Life operates on two levels. The higher level is your calling or work level. The lower level is the material or resistance level. The lower level stops us from reaching our higher level. We must stop resisting and do the work necessary to reach the higher level."
-Steven Pressfield

Resistance could mean hesitation, doubt, and fear. It could mean indecision. It could mean safety and comfort. It can also mean spending in excess on material goods. Resistance will always keep us cozy and warm but will never fulfill us. It's an insincere ally that can ultimately hurt us in the end. We may think that being safe and secure is the best way to live, but in reality, it kills our creativity and our growth. It keeps us from improving ourselves and our finances. It stifles our expansion and our ambition. When we become mature, we realize that we must be okay living with what we already have. Our talents and skills. Our possessions. Our families and communities. We don't need to look outside ourselves for approval or for acceptance. We must find our inner voice and follow what it tells us to do. As women, we have strong intuitions, but rarely use them. We must follow our instincts even if it's scary and takes us in a completely different place. That different place is closer to your purpose and closer to your higher level.

What can you do today to take a step closer to your higher level?

December 14th

"Your life is limited, so don't waste it living someone else's life."
-Steve Jobs

We don't know how much time we have on this Earth. Nobody knows when and how we will die. So why would we waste one single hour, one single day living our life that doesn't make us happy? If we're not living the way we want to live, we must immediately make a change. Nobody remembers their great, great, great, great grandparents. We may be lucky enough to have photos of them or stories that have survived the generations. But in reality, we don't know how they lived. If they loved their lives. If they were happy. All that we know is that they lived and died and that's about it. You will be remembered that way too. You may be lucky to have two generations meeting you and that's it. So why waste your time not making your life exactly the way you want? Why would you waste a single minute suffering? If there's something you hate, get rid of it. If you don't like doing something, don't do it anymore. If there's someone in your life that bugs you, get rid of them. Nothing is worth being unhappy with the precious time you're alive.

Today's challenge is to fill your day with your favorite things.

December 15th

"A woman is never sexier than when she is comfortable in her clothes."
-Vera Wang

People are drawn to others who are confident. This can be felt when they walk in the room. This can be heard when they talk about a topic of interest. This can be seen with how they carry themselves and their body language. Attractiveness and sexiness have nothing to do with beauty and everything to do with presence. When you are optimistic and assured that your product, service, advice, look, and advice are correct, then others will listen to you. Being comfortable in your own body, the way you look, and your voice inside all lead to a woman's success. Many women shy away from their confident self, leading to mundane and uneventful lives. But the ones that embrace their inner strength, know how to show the world who they are and they grab the world by its horns and enjoy the ride. Find out who you are and live your life by your principles.

What do you feel confident about?

December 16th

"The great gift of human beings is that we have the power of empathy."
-Meryl Streep

Being empathetic is a way to understand what others are feeling and thinking. It's putting ourselves in their shoes. The ability of being empathetic to others helps to give us humility in our own lives and in our own circumstances. It helps us realize that our lives aren't as bad as we may think. It helps us be grateful for the things around us that love us. It helps us feel free to express our uniqueness and our creativity. Sometimes we forget about others that are going through unfortunate circumstances as we're caught up in our own nine to five jobs. But listening, understanding, and lending a helping hand to those around us, helps us get stronger. It helps us grow. It helps us be aware of our spot on the Earth. Being a leader and helping those in need is one of the blessings we can experience during our life.

What can you do today to understand and help someone else?

December 17th

"I was angered, for I had no shoes. Then I met a man who had no feet."
-Chinese Proverb

We all get caught up in our own lives. Sometimes we are exhausted physically and mentally from all of the commitments that we make on a daily basis. We spend our time mindlessly going from activity to activity without looking around and questioning why we are blindly doing them. If we could stop and take a look around, we could start to feel grateful for our lives and all of the blessings in them. When we feel grateful and lucky that we are women who have freedom to control their own minds and bodies, to be educated, to raise families with spouses that we love, it can make any woman cry. When we are grateful, we can't feel sad, angry, or entitled. We can't be jealous of what someone else has because we know that what we have is plenty and enough for us. We can't feel unworthy when we look around at all the people who love and respect us. There's always someone else who will be more beautiful and be wealthier than you are. And there's always going to be someone else who doesn't have a nice home, wonderful relationships, or even a healthy body. Reflect on these things today and think about all of the wonderful things that are in your life.

What are the blessings in your life?

December 18th

"A fit, healthy body, that is the best fashion statement."
-Jess C Scott

It's almost the holiday season. Most of us will spend our time during the next couple of weeks going to office parties and spending a lot of time with family and friends. During those parties and get-togethers, we'll be surrounded with a lot of good food and alcoholic beverages. Even though we're in a celebratory atmosphere doesn't mean we need to get crazy and indulge in every little thing that comes our way. Most people gain a few pounds during the holidays because of their lack of discipline to their diets and exercise routines. As the cold weather approaches, it's even more important to stay on our eating and exercise regimens in order to keep ourselves looking and feeling our best. A little fun is okay, but losing focus on our health goals is not the way to start a brand new year.

What's your plan for staying healthy during the holidays?

December 19th

"The individual who says it is not possible should move out of the way of those doing it."
- Tricia Cunningham

Anything is possible if you believe it is and you start taking action to make it happen. Nothing in life will be handed to you. A great body takes a lot of effort and focus. Great finances take a lot of discipline and knowledge. A long lasting, wonderful relationship takes a lot of grace and compromise. Anything is possible if you put in the work. Every day won't be perfect. Sometimes there will be obstacles. Sometimes it will take longer to achieve your goal than you think. But that doesn't mean it's impossible. No matter who you are, where you're from, or what you have to offer, there's an opportunity for you to take just around the corner. Surround yourself with big thinkers and you too will start to think big. Surround yourself with people that are achieving great things and you too will start to achieve great things. Your network is your net worth so choose your comrades and peer group wisely.

What's possible for you?

December 20th

"What you do today can improve all your tomorrows." -*Ralph Marston*

Rome wasn't built in a day and neither will your future plans. When we decide on a goal, we can then take the first step in achieving that goal. Then another one. Then another one, until we hit our target. It will take time, discipline, and a lot of action in order to build the future we want to live in. If we want to lose weight, we must focus on less calories in and more calories out. If we want to build wealth, we must make a budget and spend less than we make in order to invest the rest. If we want to be a great mother, we must spend the time today focusing on our children. If we want a better relationship with our spouse, we need to be honest with them and get on the same page so you can build your lives together as a team and not separately. Day by day can help you build a wonderful life. Make the most of it.

What can you do today to make tomorrow better?

____

____

____

December 21st

"A friend is someone who knows all about you and still loves you."
-Elbert Hubbard

A true friend loves you no matter what. As we get older, we tend to socialize less because we're focused on raising our families. We tend to get involved with our children's activities and don't have a lot of time to spend with our girlfriends. It's a sad reality but a true one. But a true friend understands this because she's going through the same things in her life. She's always there if you need her. She'll listen to you when you need someone to talk to. She'll cry with you. She'll laugh with you. And she'll drink with you when you need something with a kick. No matter how much time goes by, a true friend is someone that doesn't miss a beat. She understands when life gets in the way of your plans. She works you in when she can spare a minute. True friendship is a treasure and helps to make life bearable when it gets tough. Make sure you have a couple of true girlfriends in your life.

Who are your dearest friends? Text them and plan a GNO (Girls' Night Out).

December 22nd

"Don't just say you have read books. Show that through them you have learned to think better, to be a more discriminating and reflective person. Books are the training weights of the mind. They are very helpful, but it would be a bad mistake to suppose that one has made progress simply by having internalized their contents."

– Epictetus, *The Art of Living: The Classical Manual on Virtue, Happiness and Effectiveness*

What are you reading right now? Are you implementing what you're reading or are you just scrolling through the words with no intention? There's so much wisdom buried in books. We're lucky that people took the time and energy to record their knowledge on every subject known to man. From science to science fiction. From self help to accounting. From gardening to painting, you can find the know-how to pursue any skillset or hobby that you desire. And the cool thing about all of this knowledge is that most of it is free through your local library. You must ask yourself if you're taking advantage of all the wealth of knowledge that's out there for you to use or are you wasting the opportunity? Most people hate school because they study things that they're not interested in. As adults, we have the privilege and freedom to read and learn about things that we want to pursue. Whether it's something fun like a hobby to something more serious like a promotion, books hold the key to our improvement in life.

What are you reading right now? Are you implementing the knowledge?

December 23rd

"Patience is bitter, but its fruit is sweet."
-Aristotle

We live in an on-demand world. Everything is at our fingertips. We can eat through a drive thru. We can skip commercials. We can binge watch series. We can buy anything we want at a touch of a finger and it shows up at our door within a day or two. But life isn't on-demand. Sometimes we must wait for things to happen. Sometimes it takes time to change a habit or achieve a goal we've been working on. In order to keep on the right path, we must show patience. Obstacles and distractions will cross our path. People won't do what they're supposed to do. We'll feel frustrated and disappointed. This is life and we must exercise not only patience but perseverance in order to live a fulfilling and meaningful life. The less we worry about the things we can't control and concentrate on the things we can, will only decrease our anxiety and stress. When life's not stressful, it seems to go the way we want. It's easier and less bumpy.

How can you show more patience?

December 24th

"As a well spent day brings happy sleep, so life well used brings happy death."
- Leonardo da Vinci

Our lives are meant to be lived. That means we should be doing as much as we can every day to live our lives to the fullest. Our lives are made up of days that are either spent wisely or spent foolishly. So what are you doing today? We should laugh today. We should feel gratitude for all the people that are in our lives. We should feel humble. We should choose an activity that can get us one step closer to our main goal. We should take some time to dream and think. We should spend some time with our family and some sexy time with our spouse. We should find a meme and text our friends something funny. We should organize something. We should clean something. We should prepare a healthy meal. We should take a walk. We should read something meaningful. When we fill our days with purpose, we spend our lives that way we want.

How are you spending your day?

December 25th

"Every time you smile at someone, it is an action of love, a gift to that person, a beautiful thing."
-Mother Theresa

Today is a special holiday for all practicing Christians and Catholics. Today is celebrated with faith, family, and friends. We gather at church and in our grandmother's homes spending time with those that we love. We reflect on the good that fills the world and the hope for a better tomorrow. We take pride in our accomplishments and in the love that surrounds us. Whatever bothers us or puts weight on our hearts, we put aside on this special day. Today we smile and delight in the fact that we're alive and that we're living in God's grace. No matter our circumstances, we have hope that things will get better. Hope that we will do better next time. Hope that we can live up to our potential. It's impossible to feel hate and love at the same time. It's impossible to be afraid and confident at the same time. It's impossible to play the victim and be successful at the same time. Take today and reflect on the positives of your life that melt your heart and make you smile.

Merry Christmas! What makes you smile?

December 26th

"Happiness is when what you think, what you say, and what you do are in harmony."
-Mahatma Gandhi

Do you have regrets? Do you have resentment? Are you telling the truth on how you really feel? Are you living the life you want? If not, you're not in alignment and you can never be truly happy. Happiness comes from within. You can't depend on outside circumstances going the way you want to be happy. You can't depend on your spouse to act the way you want to feel happy. Things aren't going to go your way. People are going to disappoint you. That's how life goes. But that doesn't mean you can have a hopeful attitude. That doesn't mean you can't be positive. That doesn't mean that you can't give others the benefit of the doubt. If you live life on your terms, there's no way you can't be happy. You can't be frustrated and happy at the same time. You can't be disappointed and happy at the same time. Think, say, and do things that allow you to feel fulfilled and happiness will naturally come into your life. It's your life, live it to its fullest and feel happiness and joy every day.

What are you thinking, saying, and doing to make yourself happy?

December 27th

"The secret of change is to focus all of your energy not on fighting the old, but on building the new."
-Socrates

In order to change, we must become a different person. In order to change, we must give something up. In order to change, we must focus our attention on different things. In order to change, we must take different actions that will give us the results we want. In order to change, we must change. We can't argue our way there. We can't take the shortcut path. We can't just imagine it or wish for it, we must take action and start moving in the direction of our goals. We must stop believing a certain way and open our minds to new and different things. We must focus on progress, taking one step at a time, and not get hung up on perfecting every step. As women, we love to change our appearance. Different nail polish, different hair colors, different clothes. Why not change the big things in our lives? A different job? A different way of handling money and investing? A different network of people to hang out with? A different method of building relationships? A different approach to motherhood. We all have the capabilities to make the changes we want to see in our lives. But we can't fight the old thoughts and ideas, we must adopt new ones and implement them and replace the old ones.

What new changes will you build today?

December 28th

"People often say that motivation doesn't last. Neither does bathing–that's why we recommend it daily."
–Zig Ziglar

How we do anything is how we do everything. If it's worth doing one day, it's worth doing every day. Practicing your craft. Improving your skills. Exercising. Eating every meal following your diet. Having great sex. Listening. Helping your children. Calling your mom. Every day we should be working on improvement. Every day we should be working on your goals. Every day we should be getting a little better. One day at a time. One step at a time until we reach the pinnacle of success. But it all starts with one day. It all starts with today. Make it great.

What step can you take today to improve your life?

December 29th

My happiness is not the means to any end. It is the end. It is its own goal. It is its own purpose."
– Ayn Rand, *Anthem*

I'll be happy when... Have you ever said that before? We all have. Instead of waiting for something to happen, why can't we just be happy along the way? Why can't we enjoy the ride to our destination? Why can't we look around and be grateful for the moment we're in right now? It's possible to be happy right now. No matter what you're going through, there's a silver lining in every dark cloud. Be aware of it and rejoice in the fact that you're here recognizing it and focus on the positive side. Releasing the worry, doubt, and anxiousness of a situation will truly set you free.

Are you happy right now? What can you do to be happy today?

December 30th

"It's not at all that we have too short a time to live, but that we squander a great deal of it. Life is long enough, and it's given in sufficient measure to do many things if we spend it well."
-Seneca, *On the Shortness of Life.*

Most women must multitask just to get through our daily life. We take on three different projects at work at the same time. We juggle doing chores at home with running our kids to soccer practice. Laundry, exercise, sex, and dishes. And this is only Monday! Before we know it, our kids are going off to college and our marriage is ending because we've lost touch with our spouse. We end up middle aged and alone because we squandered the time we had with the ones we love. This is a wake up call to all women! Stop and enjoy your family. Stop and give your best to one project at work at a time. Stop doing things half-assed because you don't have the energy or mental capacity to do it all. No one said you must be a superwoman! The women's movement gave us freedom to live our best lives. But that doesn't mean that you must give your life to everyone else. Stop and smell the roses! The dishes can wait. The laundry can wait. You don't have to do everything yourself. Ask for help. No, demand help from others. Your family can help you with the chores. Your coworkers who have been slacking can help you with the project. Take care of yourself and your needs first and then give your energy and time to others.

What will you do today to live your best day?

December 31st

"Frame your thoughts like this, you are an old person, you won't let yourself be enslaved by this any longer, no longer pulled like a puppet by every impulse, and you'll stop complaining about your present fortune or dreading the future."
-Marcus Aurelius, *Meditations- 2.2.*

Anger. Worry. Anxiousness. Fear. These are typical emotions that we as women face every day. But is there something in our life that's really that bad? Are we in physical danger? Are we worried about something that doesn't have a high probability of happening? Why do we constantly use our energy imagining the worst case scenario? Stop it! If you had a terminal diagnosis and knew you only had a short time to live, would you be worrying or anxious about something? No, you would want to spend as much time and energy doing things you've always wanted to do with the people that you love and want to spend time with. So why don't you start acting this way now? Control the things you can control and let the rest be as it may. Don't waste your precious moments in fear, or worry, or doubt, or anxiousness. Tomorrow is the start of a new year. Spend those precious moments having fun, laughing, and relaxing. That's how to live your life to its fullest by enjoying the time you have on this Earth. Get ready for the new year and the new you.

What are you worrying about today? Realize that you're anxious and think of something that you're grateful for and focus on that instead. Start tomorrow and the new year fresh and eager to make a change. How can you be ready to make next year the best year ever?

Goals for the New Year

What do you have to give up to succeed in those goals?

What do you have to change?

What opportunities are right in front of you?

Who can help you?

About the Author

Stephanie Aldrich is a general dentist, speaker, trainer, entrepreneur, and author of five other books and programs, including *There's No Crying in the Man's World*, *Nothing But the Tooth: 11 Question You Should Ask Your Dentist*, *The Habit Formula: Life's Success Equation*, *The Habit Formula: A Parent's Success Equation Kid's Edition*, *The Backward Rule: The Ultimate Way to Hit Any Target*, and *The 9 Truths: Don't f*ck up your life.*

Coming from humble beginnings in a small town in Ohio, Dr. Aldrich continues to strive for success for not only herself and her companies but also for others. Knowing that anything is possible drives her creativity to handle issues plaguing individuals and companies. When you start with the individual and what's in it for them, you can implement change that trickles down to the company as a whole.

Dr. Aldrich lives in Copley, Ohio, with her loving husband, Steven, and their wonderful son, Noah.

www.ingramcontent.com/pod-product-compliance
Lightning Source LLC
LaVergne TN
LVHW020524100826
845148LV00010B/1333